The Last Wild Edge

The Last Wild Edge

One Woman's Journey
from the Arctic Circle
to the Olympic Rain Forest

Susan Zwinger

Johnson Books
BOULDER

Published in the United States by Johnson Books, a division of Johnson Publishing Company, 1880 South 57th Court, Boulder, Colorado 80301. E-mail: books@jpcolorado.com

9 8 7 6 5 4 3 2 1

Cover design by Debra B. Topping
Cover illustration by Jane Zwinger
Front matter map by James Lee Roth

Library of Congress Cataloging-in-Publication Data
Zwinger, Susan, 1947–
    The last wild edge: one woman's journey from the Arctic Circle to the Olympic rain forest / [Susan Zwinger].
        p.   cm.
    ISBN 1-55566-241-2 (paper: alk. paper)
    1. Yukon Territory—Description and travel. 2. Northwest, Pacific—Description and travel. 3. Arctic regions—Description and travel. 4. Zwinger, Susan, 1947– —Journeys—Yukon Territory. 5. Zwinger, Susan, 1947– —Journeys—Northwest, Pacific. 6. Zwinger, Susan, 1947– —Journeys—Arctic regions. I. Title.
F1091.Z95   1999
917.19—dc21   98-52744
                                                                            CIP

Printed in the United States by
Johnson Printing
1880 South 57th Court
Boulder, Colorado 80301

 Printed on recycled paper with soy ink

To all the western red cedars, western hemlocks,
Douglas firs, black spruce, and Sitka spruce
who sheltered me

Contents

Preface

$\mathcal{E}$ dges, those paradoxical meshes of boundary and beckoning; I had always loved edges. My life had folded in the middle, like the tarp draped across the tree branch that just then sheltered me from rain. As I listened to oversized rain drops plopping from the red cedar above me, I craved nothing short of a comprehensive, epic myth by which to understand my forest homeland and myself. I needed the poetry of Earth to resuscitate me, not an armchair treatise but a sphagnum-bog-mucky, seat-of-the-pants revelation. Rootlessness had robbed me of a sense of meaning and belonging. I wanted to replace mind-dumbing words such as sound bite, countdown, boot up, and HOVs with sensually resonant words: wolverine, bog rosemary, boletus, grizzly, sphagnum, and glacial cirque. I needed to travel out to an edge and beyond—an edge both metaphorical and literal.

As an Air Force child and, later, an artist and a teacher, I had lived in seventeen different states by midlife. I longed for an intimate knowledge of one landscape and one region.

As a transient, I am representative of humankind. Human history *is* migration toward a chain of "last wild edges" called frontiers. The western edge of North America is a final edge to settle on a finite planet. Where does humankind go from here? Where else have we not settled, altered, and consumed? I suspect that Europeans saved this wild edge for last because its geography is punched, exploded, ground, and drenched. Its forest of enormous trees has created a boundary difficult to penetrate, let alone farm.

Major migration to North America could just as well have arrived from the opposite direction. Using the first mariner's compass (invented by his people), the Chinese admiral and explorer Zheng He traveled to East Africa beginning in 1405. With expeditions including as many as sixty-two ships carrying twenty-eight thousand men and animals, he had the capability to reach America and beat Columbus by almost a century.[1] Why didn't the Chinese conquer the wild western shores of North America and its small bands of nature-symbiotic humans? Manifest destiny, European superiority? Musk ox manure. Geography and natural history forge human history.

The great coastal mountain ranges—the Alaskan, the Wrangellian, the Cordilleran, the Cascadian, the Olympian—created entire weather systems, which created ecosystems of their own. These, in turn, helped write the history of human migration. Early man found it easier to spread through Europe and Asia and then later brave the Atlantic Ocean to the new continent than to penetrate the ragged, young mountain ranges of what would become Alaska and British Columbia.

My own journeys stretched over twelve years and eighteen degrees latitude from the Arctic Circle in the Yukon to the Hoh River mouth on Washington's Pacific Coast. I traveled in spurts, not in a logical order. To write about my journeys, I rearranged them into a coherent order running from north to south. This allowed me to examine how the lush temperate forests of North America reappear after an icy demolition.

I traveled by pickup, by day hike, by sailboat, by Zodiac™, by kayak, and by strapping on a pack and slogging out beyond toilets, televisions, and other human beings. Backpacking is one of the finest forms of storytelling: The landscape is a lifelong sequence of tales. The animals, plants, minerals, oceans, and atmosphere become my lexicon; the ecosystem, my syntax.

My story begins with a solitary trek through the Yukon Territories and continues as I join five Canadians to sail on a small boat down

---

[1] Gould, Stephen Jay, "Second-Guessing the Future," *Natural History,* September 1998, 20–29, 64–66.

the Hecate Lowlands of coastal British Columbia, through bogs and immense rain forests. We sailed in and out of the vast fjord system to document pristine territory that was about to be clearcut with the blessing of the Canadian "Ministre" of Forests.

Next, I camped my way south along a fragment of the lost continent of Cascadia, Vancouver Island, amid some of the most magnificent trees left on Earth. On Meares Island, I found trees sixty feet around. Ferrying from Vancouver Island to the Olympic Peninsula, a landmass formed of lava heaved up from the ocean bottom, I climbed to the center of its unique, circular mountain range. From the icy skirts of Mount Olympus, I backpacked eighteen miles down from Blue Glacier through the Hoh rain forest toward the Hoh River mouth. My journey ended on the south end of the longest wilderness beach left in the Lower Forty-Eight.

The Politics of Size: The Forest's Whistle-Blowers

"To slow down, to kneel down, to gaze long" can be understood as a political act, as well as a vegetative genuflection. When reading the descriptions of my journeys, some friends suggested that I remove the passages describing the ecology of small organisms—the functioning of lichen, the balances of liverwort, and the interconnections of fungal mycelia—and replace them with environmental politics. The cryptogams and mycorrhizal fungus *are* my rabble-rousers. Without them, no forest grows for long.

I did not want to write another treatise about the planetary giants, the sexy megafauna at the top of the food chain. I roar on behalf of the lowly beings that have the tenacity and flexibility to begin life over again—and again and again—and the energy to crank a huge ecosystem. Though my journey culminated among arboreal giants in a forest capable of producing the greatest biomass per hectare on the planet, I never lost sight of the cryptogams.

Because the cryptogams gather much of their sustenance from the air and are sensitive to pollution, these small organisms are the whistle-blowers signaling the ill health of the whole ecosystem. A complete world exists aloft in the forest canopy. In a mature, temperate rain forest, epiphytes (lichen, mosses, fungus, liverworts, and club mosses) can account for thousands of pounds of plant matter per acre. Pollution-sensitive lobaria lichens will not grow near cities. The mycorrhizae, which weave together healthy old forests underground, are not easily regenerated after slash and burn. A single old Douglas fir may hold over sixty million needles weighing some 440 pounds with a surface area for holding water of almost an acre.[2] Epiphytes have evolved to hold many times their weight in water. Removing those needles and their load of lichens and mosses shifts the local moisture regime toward rapid runoff, flooding, and ironically, drought. Within and without these needles, symbiotic fungi feed millions of insects that, in turn, support a large bird population. Without these unseen fungi, the aviary dwindles. Rachel Carson's silence.

To know the landscape intimately and not just pass through, each one of us must develop the vibrissae of a vole, the nose of a fox, the ears of an owl, the chemical-sensing mycelia of a truffle, the echolocation of a bat, the directional sense of an arctic tern, and the eyes of a bald eagle. These journeys taught me that I needed heart, as well as legs, knees, and a hand lens, to discover the world in a centimeter of lichen and the circumference of a mountain.

---

[2] Chris Maser, *Forest Primeval: The Natural History of an Ancient Forest* (San Francisco: Sierra Club Books, 1989), 99.

Acknowledgments

I wish to thank the thousands of forest activists in Canada, the United States, and Europe who have written letters, called their representatives, or put their bodies in front of logging trucks to oppose the massive destruction of our forests, as well as everyone who passes on their love of the wild places to children.

Many thanks to those whose minds filter through rain forests: Among them, Joe Foy of the Western Canada Wilderness Coalition, Fred Rhoades, Dave Shaw, Ruth Kirk, Bob Steelquist, Paul Crawford, and the many National Park Service employees taught me a great deal. I would like to thank my crew of local readers: Susan Scott, Anne Davenport, Winnie Adams, Jim Lux, Marian Blue, Wayne Ute, Celeste Mergens, Joni Takanikos, Barton Cole, and Susan Favor, as well as all the employees of the small but excellent Sno-Isle Public Library System. And I want to thank all those in the extended Natural History family, especially writers Ann Zwinger, Parker Huber, John Daniel, Gary Nabhan, Bob Pyle, and Tim McNulty, who have cheered me on whenever I have decided that natural history writing is clearly dysfunctional behavior.

Facing West from California's shores,
Inquiring, tireless, seeking what is yet unfound,
I, a child, very old, over waves towards house of
    maturity, the land of migrations, look afar,
Look off the shores of my Western sea, the circle
    almost circled;
For starting westward from Hindustan, from the vales
    of Kashmere,
From Asia, from the north, from the God, the sage,
    the hero,
From the south, from the flowery peninsulas and
    the spice islands,
Long having wander'd since, round the earth having
    wander'd,
Now I face home again, very pleas'd and joyous.
(But where is what I started for so long ago?
And why is it yet unfound?)

    —Walt Whitman, "Facing West from California's Shores"

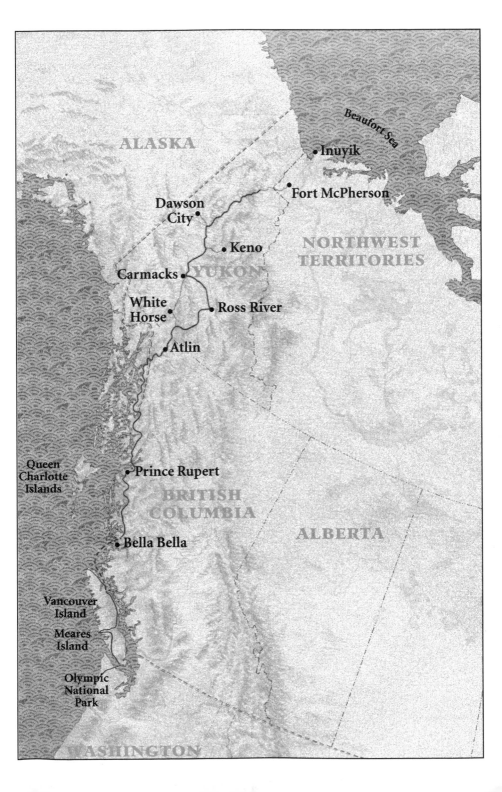

The Last Wild Edge

Part One

From the Arctic Circle to the Alaskan Coast

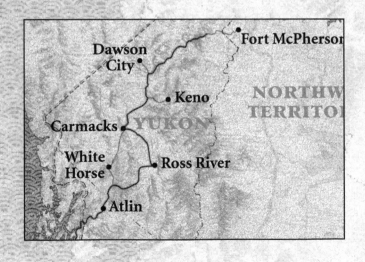

Land of
No Trees at All

66°45' N

*I*ndistinguishable ripples the size of Kansas. I am sitting all alone above the Arctic Circle in a September snow flurry.

Tundra. At first I know only monotony. The tundra rolls out endlessly, covered in a low carpet of rusts, reds, greens, browns, and purple. No trees break the horizon. Nothing at all breaks the horizon. I feel a white man's fear of being lost forever in howling space. I cannot line up distant objects to travel a certain direction. No perspective. Samuel Johnson wrote of the Scottish Highlands that an eye accustomed to flowery pastures and waving harvest is astonished and repelled by such a wide extent of hopeless sterility.

Despairing, I close my eyes for a long time. The wind drills through my body. I forget everything I know. After two hours, my eyes spring open: There, in great splendor, is the tundra.

Impatience gone, I perceive the tundra a little bit more as an Inuit must see it: at once magic; at once a vast, disperse supermarket on wing, hoof, root, and fin; at once a sink for human souls. I now see that there are dots all over this tundra. Some are alive. A long time watching teaches me which are plants and which are caribou and which are cairns. The tundra becomes intriguing. Then it becomes animated. Then, with enough time, the land is vibrating with gustatory and spiritual possibilities. The sun glows, fifty degrees, no shadows. The tundra flattens.

The tundra's human-dwarfing vastness requires more humility

3

than I yet have. With voids the size of Montana and temperature ranging from Nebraska to Pluto, the tundra remains close to the primal state of our planet. An open book.

The human beings who evolved as part of the Arctic ecosystem believe that spirits are entrapped within outcrops. Some spirits are dangerous, a soul trapped in stone anxious to get out. Some are enticing, helpful spirits. If this were my "home" landscape, each landmark would have a story: "I walked this way when … "; "I was almost out of water when … "; "I saw my first vermilion flycatcher with my lover when … "; and so on. The landforms here have names and stories that set the trail and create the map. I just don't know them yet.

As an artist who documents the natural world, I should be visually astute by default. However, the Inuit has visual acuity far beyond my own. His life depends on it. A mental map-making ability depends not only upon visual acuity, but upon *retention*. Up here, the detail smooshes together in my memory, and I forget.

I could wander this way or that way and always find something new. Something edible or something curious. From where I sit, a human being could spread out infinitely in every direction, even up or down. Even backwards through time. Up here, for those Inuit who have never been airborn and for myself, there is no geometric grid based on an aerial view and Renaissance painting concept. Space is measured in time: three days by snowmobile up to Old Crow, five days to the place where seals are hunted.

Time and space interchange here, not just from within the Inuit world view but in the reality of the land. When I lived in New Mexico, I learned about cyclical time from the Hopi. Liquid time, dry time, frozen time, spiral time. Time being inextricably connected with Earth events. It requires weeks to begin to perceive the land this way.

Inuit hunters measure distance not in miles but in overnights. So do I: As a backpacker, I measure out my food exactly, according to the number of days and nights I expect my journey will last. The Inuit know that time is a dimension of distance. Distance is a fusion of weather, visibility, ground type, quality of human attentiveness, and how much one's dreams are fulfilled. In my small art notebook, I draw "reality" maps, complex layerings of detail. Reality is not geometric in these maps.

When it comes to time, I am stubborn. Digital-clock time shoots into European Americans like a staple gun shoots staples onto rigid frames. After a long time, I finally give up my old perception of time. My imagination spreads out in all directions, exchanging time for space. I take out my compass and travel toward a rocky form on the horizon that catches my fancy. As I walk toward it balancing my boots on the higher mounds above the water-filled sphagnum, the rock transforms into a troll, then into a nutmeg grinder, and finally into an up-ended vortex. Gazing back with caribou eyes, I spy a human dot on the land where I just sat. A dangerous dot.

I travel forward for an hour and forty minutes. I want to say "about four miles," but mileage has no meaning. The land expands and contracts constantly. My senses are keened by the potentiality of grizzly and other curious beings. If it were cloudy and later in the fall, there would be other data to guide me: The clouds would reflect open bodies of water and snow-free land beneath them. *Sastrugi*, or hard snow-wind ridges, could lead me in the direction of the prevailing winds. It is the way I read the desert dunes when I am confused in the middle of them: studying the prevailing wind direction and how I must move in relationship to it.

Here, finally, is space for the soul to travel that ever-expanding funnel of lines depicting the magnetic fields off the top pole of the Earth. Such vastness is long gone in the Lower Forty-Eight; the wilderness frontier there was declared dead in 1894.

The tundra holds the elixir of otherness. In tundra, I find the poetry of desert.

I grew up with southwestern deserts oozing into my brain by osmosis. In tundra, I find traits from the Sonoran. Stooping to pour warm canteen water on a "dead" lichen, I watch it unfurl into life. Here, as in the Sonoran, the dusky-red and lavender plants turn the horizon rusts and purples. The purple pigment indicates anthocyanin, which protects a plant from ultraviolet rays here and in the Southwest. Anthocyanin is an extraordinary evolutionary invention: A rich protein, it stores nourishment while the plant is dormant and allows it to spring into growth as soon as there is enough water, warmth, or whatever is lacking.

Both desert and tundra are Pulvinate Cosmos: miles and miles of low, dome-shaped plants. The pulvinate form results from the evolutionary shrinking of a plant into a tight pincushion, which creates a warmer microclimate within. A tall, showy lupine in Texas shrinks, over thousands of years, to a five-inch-high dome covered with minute pink bonnets above timberline. In the desert and tundra, the wind creates protective teardrop shapes in the lee of each obstacle. Snarled, dead leaves left from the previous year create a tent for new life. Even under the snow, the plant starts to grow by creating its own greenhouse effect through warmth from its metabolism.

The shrinking, fattening, or toughening of leaves, the chemical tainting for inedibility, the dwarfing to minimize resource use: all this I have grown to love on the desert. All this is here in the Arctic.

Two of the five American deserts, the Arctic and the Sonoran, spiritually belong to those people who have evolved within them: the Inuits here, the O'odham Tohono Hia-Ced on the Arizona-Mexico border. Both have survived one of the harshest climates on Earth through keen attunement to, and recognition of, their symbiosis with the fragile biosphere. Both will have much to teach us about surviving on a fragile margin of life if we insist upon reproducing willy-nilly.

It is cold now. Having driven southward for an unknown number of miles, I stand near a remote Inuviakuktun outpost and watch out of my peripheral vision as a young mother scrapes a skin in front of her prefab shelter. Semifrozen animal carcasses and parts are piled up in the yard. I try not to stare, but what I see is so alien to my temperate-climate cleanliness that I am fascinated. Periodically she cuts off a hunk of flesh and chews it up for her new baby. How can she live in this vast treelessness? As she holds the little one to her breast, she is telling the tundra's stories with her heartbeat, stomach, memory, and milk.

In ironic ways, the young Inuit mother is no longer isolated from large population centers. Pollution from eastern Europe pours over the North Pole each winter. Although the Arctic Coast is about as far as one can imagine from the industrial sewers and smokestacks of eastern Europe, scientists have measured an increasing array of toxic pollutants within the Arctic food chain in the last thirty years. Heavy metals and chemicals from industry, pesticides from agriculture, and radioactive fallout from Chernobyl are found in ice, snow, water, air, and on all levels of the Arctic food chain—plankton to polar bear.

These isolated people live largely off the sea by hunting seals, whales, birds, and other wildlife: large amounts of food from near the top of the food chain. Due to biomagnification, their food exposes them to higher levels of contaminants than other North Americans experience. Chemicals and heavy metals become more concentrated as they move up the trophic chain. For instance, polychlorinated biphenyls (PCBs), which accumulate in the fatty tissue of zooplankton, increase in concentration by two million times by the time they reach the large marine mammals.

Yet the Inuits must continue to eat their native foods. Whale and seal blubber and caribou fat are delicacies to the Inuit. Traditional food is richer by far in nutrients and far cheaper than processed food sent in from the south, and it is a traditional part of the Inuit spiritual life.[1]

How I longed to arrive in a spot on the planet that is so remote, it remains untouched by the dominant culture and its industries. I don't find that here. Pollutants from around the world are being carried north by rivers, ocean currents, and weather systems in winter. A

---

[1] Karen Twitchell, "The Not-So-Pristine Arctic," *Canadian Geographic* 180 (Feb.–March 1991): 53–60.

hard travelers' lesson to learn, this giving up of the romance of the North.

Far to the north of the young mother's house, the wind blows steadily in from the Arctic Ocean uncovering human-arranged, six-foot wide stone rings on the tundra, the same type as the ancient tent rings used for thousands of years. The young mother's brothers and uncles still cover great distances to reason with the seal and walrus and narwhal, to perform rituals and humbly summon these magnificent Sea People to give up their bodies temporarily to feed human families. All animals, they know, have souls that are keenly attuned to the intentions of man. It is our great loss as contemporary urbanites to be so brutally removed from the animals whose souls we borrow that we no longer carry on such discourse. Even when I do meet a chicken, I feel little urge toward discourse. With the Inuit, through careful ceremony, all the seal souls will be returned, sailed out to sea in seal bladders to reenter seal pup bodies.

Although the Inuit remain inextricably bound to plants and animals, modern tools are integrated into their everyday life: snowmobiles, synthetic clothes, radios, computers. Some Inupiat Eskimo of both countries support the petroleum industry because it has radically changed their Third World lifestyle into that of a well-endowed American. Here in Canada, the Inuit Nation owns the oil company. Although oil can raise the average Far North Inuit family income far above the income level to the south, such a lifestyle will be hard to maintain when the oil is gone. Oil has changed the Inuit life radically: for better and for worse.

Daily, curious white people arrive in sports utility vehicles or by tour plane, seeking the clichés by which we fantasize the Far North. Simply by coming we tie the Inuit to the rest of the world. Although the vast, icy tundra is still an effective physical moat from civilization below, the soul of a global human peers from each coppery face.

Land of Scrawny Trees
and Huge Miracles

We all travel the Milky Way together—trees and men.
—John Muir

66°33' N

$\mathcal{I}$ awaken on September 13 to find the world absolutely blank except for two black eyes moving. For a frightening moment, I cannot figure out why all is stark white and the tundra has gone. It is so cold, every limb I move seems to freeze. To warm up the propane in my camp stove to the point where it will light, I grab the stove and hold it between my legs. My bone marrow is frozen. Snow is solid in the air.

A total whiteout. A blank sheet of photographic paper. Above the Arctic Circle, sixty-six degrees thirty-three minutes north, I lie in a black pickup near the Continental Divide in the Richardson Mountains. My only reality is the six-foot by four-foot by four-foot aluminum and steel box whose volume I have reduced by half with a kitchen, library, bed, and camping gear. I squirm around to the back window, careful not to let even an inch of bare shoulder slip from its down cocoon. The back canopy window is solid with an icy fern forest grown from my body's night moisture. The thermometer says eight degrees, and it's already been warming up for an hour.

My own death lurks out there on soft, downy ptarmigan feet, as lovely as it is unseen. Hypothermia is a peaceful death: First to sleep, then to dream, and then nothingness. Not Sartre's philosophic Nothingness but a deep, infinite void, dark as the outer edge of the universe.

Yet, I am not frightened. Not because of the illusions of civilization I carry—boxes of stove fuel to melt snow, boxes of dried powders in small foil envelopes decorated with lush photographs of vegetables, animal parts, and spices. No, my peace is in the comfort of edges. Exploratory humans find a perverse pleasure in going to the edge of the known, opening the door, looking down into the deep muck of chaos, and then, with thumb on nose, fingers waggling, giving it one great hell of a send-off.

This edge is draped over the Richardson Mountains, a bleak, low, Icelandic range of gray sediment, now covered with the winter's first snow. From here, the fate of each rivulet is decoded: north to the Arctic Ocean or south to the Yukon River, then west to the Bering Sea. I think that I am the only thing alive for miles and years and miles. My own death would be just another natural recycling of an organic blip back into the spirals of nature. Nothing to get all worked up about. But my solitude is far, far from real.

Frozen chips of sky swirl around. Nearby, out in the whiteness, arrives a reverberating musical croak tuning itself up in pitch increments like gears of ebony wood cranking loudly. Black and polished, this sound comes out of the whiteout like a fist from a sleeve.

Raven!

From Mexico to the Yukon, the mythic raven is one crazy bird, one of the very few to stay north all winter. He is also, legend has it, crazy enough to have allowed the very first human beings to crawl from another world into this one. According to the Haida, a coastal people of the Queen Charlotte Islands, Raven found a huge bivalve on Rose Spit, the northeastern end of the Haida Gwaii. Inside he heard a new sort of being scratching to get out. He sensed that this new creature meant trouble, but he was vastly curious, a trickster. He acts naïve, but he knows everything. He opened up the clam shell and let out the very first humans upon the earth. They, of course, were Haida.

The raven I was hearing croaks again and hops down from a rocky outcrop to work through the snow. I struggle on more clothes, glad for his presence. He is trying to show me something, teaching me about the snow or something underneath it. But I will have to get out of the truck bed to see it.

"Raven," I groan, pulling on another layer, "I don't want to do this."

But he won't let go. I stoop to dig through the snow where he is digging and find it warmer, much warmer, beneath. I find the very beginning of terrestrial life after a glacier: the black mat of *Alectoria* lichen.

"Clue! Clue!" croaks the raven and flaps off toward the North Pole where Earth drops away into space. I scrape away more snow with a gloved hand. This is *Alectoria nigricans*, decumbent, mottled gray with black tips, covering much of the raw rock and river cobble from here down through the Oregon coastline, growing all over Alaska and into Siberia. It is an ugly, small lichen with nothing to recommend it except that it foreshadows the great temperate rain forests.

Lichens are an essential beginning of life on stone, the first life to hold moisture, to capture nutrients from dust and air, to build soil. Along with mosses and liverworts, they are known as terrestrial cryptogams. Their soil building action, hastened by the mechanical action of frost on rock, hints of the great boreal, montane, and rain forest ecosystems to the south. Cryptogams are prevalent in the Northwest's forests, where the ground is completely covered by mosses and lichens and more hang from the canopy in long strands or form entire ecosystems high above the ground: soil and all. These humble, nonvascular plants make up much of the bulk produced by the forests.

Cryptogams! A path of hidden truths; miniature, elusive, seductive patterns.

Lichens are sagacious little beings. An extensive experiment in symbiosis, this bond of algae and fungi has reinvented itself again and again in the history of life. This bonding may have made it possible for the first plants to come out of the ocean by adding a backpack of food and moisture to the fungal structure. The algae invaded the fungi to create a new species. Currently over twenty-five thousand lichens are described, and many more as yet are unknown.

The symbiosis of algae and fungi means that lichen need neither soil nor roots to survive. The fungi offer structure, while the ten percent alga content is able to photosynthesize and then cycle nutrients back through the layers of fungi. Lichen store sugars and minerals and, because their nutrition arrives as particles in the air, are hypersensitive collectors of pollutants. The factories of eastern Europe feed the caribou heavy metals through the cladina lichens. An exact record of the industrial age, the use of leaded gasolines, Chernobyl, as well as climatic history are recorded within these lichens.

In thin, humble crusts, lichen creep over many of the inhospitable parts of our planet: walls, bare stone, graves, tree trunks, old logs, dead things, and places with little light. Able to resist drought, lichen appear to shrivel and die during dry periods only to spring to life as soon as the rains come. Temperature extremes fry and freeze lichens without causing injury. Their non-vascular structure means they have less resistance to water passing in or out. Desiccation is not a problem. Low nutrients, no sweat.

The price lichen pay for such versatile tenacity is very slow growth, one millimeter per year for some. Yet, they can live thousands of years. By measuring the growth of a particular species of lichen on surfaces of known ages, such as ancient walls and graves, humans have created time lines that are used to measure the retreat of ice on glacial moraines all over the world.

The Arctic Circle is an imaginary line around the upper sixth of the planet above which the sun does not rise at all during part of the winter. North of me, eight million square miles of icy tundra lie dormant. Permafrost close to the surface melts briefly in July and August, signaling the start of the greatest gush of high-speed life anywhere on Earth. Beneath my feet, permafrost penetrates to twelve hundred feet, where it encounters heat from Earth's core.

"Arrghxxck!" raunches the raven. I rip my lunch from a small silver package and devour it without crumbs. Did I not realize that we were locked in a cooperative relationship? Should I not share? Astute

Inuit observers have told me that the raven is capable of fruitful relationships with a number of other communicative animals, such as wolves, coyotes, dogs, other large birds, and man. The fact that I am the only large animal for miles escapes me; I take the raven's companionship as deep flattery.

The raven's call through the whiteout deeply resonates throughout the color spectrum and comforts me. Seeing far and wide, he will call out a newly dead animal on the tundra. Then, as if solely for his personal benefit, wolves will come running from afar to open the carcass so that the raven can eat. They are partners this way.

In return for this service, ravens save wolves and coyotes miles of energy-exhausting travel through deep snow. In summer, the wolf or coyote will hunt small rodents while ravens hang out in the trees above. I have frequently used a raven's ruckus to be forewarned of the presence of other animals: bighorn sheep in the Mojave and brown bear on the Kenai Peninsula, Alaska.

But what has this raven to do with my search for shrubs and trees?

The snow ceases to drift horizontally. Pale, pale sunlight vibrates through the whiteout like a Ukranian women's choir singing on adjacent notes. Soon the raven and I can see far off to the Richardson Mountains where solifluction, soil flowing downhill like molasses, has left one-hundred-foot tors, rock spires of ancient sea deposit, poking the sky. Unlike British Columbia's tumultuous coastlines, there were no glaciers here. Though it snows, it is dry in the Arctic interior; the Pacific squalls, those great slings of moisture, do not make it so far inland.

Giant mammals with their symbiont, prehistoric man, once munched through vestigial pockets of older vegetation left in the big gap where glaciers forgot to scrape. Humans slunk gingerly southward down the narrow corridor between two huge ice masses toward the marshes and lakes of Nevada and then, perhaps, on to South America. They originally followed the wooly mammoth and giant sloth south toward the humid swamps of what is now Great Basin

Desert, until they overhunted their prey. A giant sloth stood eight feet tall and had a face and physique to unnerve Darth Vader. The fossil record does not tell us if this giant moved quickly or slowly. I drive very slowly through the once again blowing snow.

Traveling in a poor man's Winnebago, a two-wheel-drive Mazda pickup and canopy, I have only four small tires and one narrow mud trough between myself and eternity. Before this "highway" was begged from the vast wilderness early this century, the entire tundra region remained a blank space on white man's maps. The first contact between white and Inuviakuktun bands happened along this route. A muddy strip of Yukon humor, the Dempster "Highway" is named after the first Royal Canadian Mountie to travel repeatedly over this route, Corporal W. D. Dempster. Unlike the Haul Road up to Prudhoe Bay, Alaska, which was quickly and crudely built and closed to the public until 1991, the Dempster entices the more adventuresome and less rational traveler.

Free eating is good. I have not shared my food, choosing not to feed wild animals or ruin their digestive tracts with freeze-dried chemicals. My companion seems to consider flying up through the roiling whiteout to the Inuviakuktun village, where animal carcasses might lie in the front yards. Flying, though, appears to be too much trouble; this bird looks cold. I watch him consider other options. He is so empty that he hears his own being buzz from ear to ear.

He spies me far below slipping out of kilter down the pass in the Richardson Mountains past the Arctic Circle. The raven detects something moving twenty miles below on Rock River. In the Rock River camp, he flies down to inspect two Inuviapik hunters, one very, very old and the other quite young, walking in from nowhere through a whiteout. I find them too and gape in amazement—no vehicle anywhere in sight. As their ancestors have for ten thousand years, they are crossing the Yukon landscape on foot. The younger one looks away from me as if I am an evil spirit. The older one's face is as dark as slate and eroded to bone. He is not glad to see me. His black eyes pierce to the back of my skull.

The raven suddenly flies south. I follow to find him hopping about on a slab of stone.

"Clue! Clue! Clue!" caws the raven.

"Okay, okay," I say, dropping to my knees. Hurting my hands in the rocky snow, I lift the slab and poke underneath. There! Curls of caribou lichen rise with a powerful pale-green life force, shaped like miniature rubber antlers. I force my fingers into the frozen earth and through the woven, unending root system that is knitting the loose mineral soil together. My companion picks at the spot where I have removed the slab, finding something to eat. Freezing wind blows up his feathers and my hair. Suddenly he knows what he needs, and I know what I need.

Trees.

I drive through the Richardson Mountains until I come to the top of a steep drop in altitude. It dawns on me that if I slide off the road, I could die up here.

Taking a deep breath, I drop three thousand feet down the pass: the raven is gliding overhead, and I am sliding somewhat out of control. Below the pass, I find the Eagle River Bridge arching rust against a powdery eggshell sky; the clouds have risen and peeled back to reveal an egg white, damp zenith. Startlingly white birch trunks reflect down into the icy brown river mirror. The bridge crosses the river upside down as well as right side up.

The blue-black raven flies into the very first cottonwood trees we've seen on our southward journey, the northern-most ranks of these trees, shimmering paler than the pale Arctic sun. I walk around with my arms unslung from my pits and touch the world. I am so grateful for these first few, slim trees.

These first trees appear fragile and beautiful, the first plants taller than people on the wind-flattened tundra. Eggshell birch bark glows against the dark steel sky, naturally peeling back to reveal a bright salmon inner layer.

Dusk lasts for a very long time. This night, tens of thousands of stars shine in the crystal-cold air. The night will be stingingly cold. I sleep soundly all night long until, with a loud bang and scrape-clack-

clack-clack, the raven lands on the truck canopy. He wants my body heat. He wants breakfast.

"Damn you, raven," I complain, sticking the freezing stove between my legs again. The raven makes a sound that sets the frozen air on fire.

Nothing to eat here!

Twelve miles down the road, more trees. I muse: "How do these first trees begin?" That they grow here at all seems miraculous. Imperceptively, the trees rose up from prostrate shrubs to a low crouch until, quite unexpectedly, they plucked themselves up from the very earth—from recumbent, dwarf birch vines into forty-foot shimmering stalks.

Treeline begins extremely slowly as individual trees, stunted and gnarled, grow singly and in small groups in the sheltered folds of a ridge. This is taiga, Russian for "land of little sticks," tilted, squatty, ratty, black spruce forests. Here, beneath our feet, begins the grandest forest on the globe, a band six thousand miles broad of great temperate forest that rings the Northern Hemisphere: from western Alaska clear to the Atlantic Coast, across the Bering Strait, through Siberia and Scandinavia, then back to me on Eagle River.

In the stinging, subzero weather, I draw inside the truck, a pupa in an aluminum cocoon.

A loud clang rings out like a shot. I jump out of my skin.

The raven has carried my cook pot to the top of the canopy to clean out the dried rinds from a freeze-dried dinner. Finding his sharp beak inconvenienced, he tosses the pot into the air like a spoiled child.

I find myself laughing out loud at him, an odd sound in this empty tundra. Strange, this bird's presence brings such profound comfort. He is so huge that he carries his own atmosphere with him like Jupiter. Each nacreous blue-black feather lies in place like an almost-decipherable cuneiform. He pulls my eyes to him like a black magnet in a land weakly hued in snow-swept tans. He walks with a dignified waddle, making commentary on the events of the world in deep musical croaks. He looks askance upon me as a recalcitrant, substandard being.

"So *why* do these trees begin at all?" I address the raven out loud. It is not the warmth of the sun that calls in the tree bones but the increasing sun time, which allows the trunks to grow tough enough to survive the winter. Even these first dwarf black spruce pull in enough light and heat for summer growth and tenuous winter survival. With deep snowdrifts persisting over half the year, the extreme cold of winter not only threatens to freeze them but sucks away precious moisture. Frozen water covers them, and permafrost holds their roots, yet no water is available to them. They face the extreme drought of deserts.

These black spruce, the dominant tree of the taiga, are vivid characters. Scrawny, sickly, and uneven branches protrude like used pipe cleaners. An exaggerated vertical spire results from hormonal suppression of branches growing laterally, thus avoiding the burden of heavy snow.

Nature designed the perfect leaf for deep cold: the needle. Snow does not weigh it down; it contains little sap to freeze. Dark green, it absorbs maximum heat from sunshine. Microscopic plates, stomata, absorb carbon dioxide and exude oxygen with much less water loss than in other plants. The stomata lie in tiny pits along the bottom of a groove; air is held still around them. Water loss is almost nil. Not elegant, these spruce. Inelegant, yet ingenious in their survival strategy.

The trees' stiff needles, seldom more than a half-inch long, are closely crunched together on all sides of slow-growing branches. Northern peoples ferment a drink from these needles that Henry David Thoreau once claimed would "acclimate and naturalize a man at once."

These trees elude and embrace death. Not only do they avoid freezing by a decrease of saturation in their membrane lipids, lowering the ice crystallization temperature, but they also do so through very active metabolic changes. Osmotically active substances, such as sugars, organic acids, and proteins, concentrate in winter to protect the trees against lethal desiccation.[1]

I, too, am evolving a grace within this cold barrenness. By adapting to forlorn landscapes, I am paradoxically gaining strength from an interior winter.

I shiver and shiver in my inadequate shells. Capilene, cotten, flannel, thick wool, down, synthetic fleece. Gathering twigs and needles for a fire, I feel the raven's eyes penetrate me like a hot oil drill. "No fire here!" I imagine him scolding. "Too many mysteries, too much effort in survival."

---

[1] Peter J. Marchand, *Life in the Cold: An Introduction to Winter Ecology* (Hanover, NH: University Press of New England, 1987), p.57.

Of Howls and Timberline

63° N, 137° W

In the middle of the night, I am awakened by a long, low moan-howl—then another and another, layered and complex. A lugubrious glow lights up the tundra beyond a few spruce silhouettes. The surface of my skin is tingling. Wolves!

At first I count five distinct individuals, but within the interference wave patterns of adjacent notes, they seem to multiply. Nothing at all like the high-pitched songs of coyotes, this song is deep, resonating from broad chests, 125-pound bodies, and wide paws that spread across the deep snow in midwinter. This howl survives at eighty degrees below zero.

But what is this light? No moon tonight. Just the pale green shimmer of silk lines in a curtain radiating down from the North Pole. All night long, I sleep on a knife's edge, waiting for that bone-hollowing song to fill me again as it announces the location of wolves or the success of a hunt, or merely the canine joy of being alive. Under the low, overcast morning sky, I begin the long drive south again, snow nipping at my tires.

The Arctic timberline stalks toward me across the tundra like a winter-wooled wolf with its fur half scraped away in the spring. The camouflage pattern of black krummholz against the red tundra creates a strange, earth-sized skin. The tree line transitional zone, the broadest ecotone on the planet, creeps north in two segments. Here, the northernmost, scattered patches of dwarfed trees huddle together in isolated, sheltered sites nestled into the matrix of tundra.

The Colorado alpine timberlines of my adolescence transformed from forest into steep scree in under a quarter mile. The much wider breadth of the polar timberline is biologically significant: Separated as far as they are, the trees cannot reproduce by seed. The hundred-mile-wide belt of on-again, off-again forest requires the black spruce to reproduce vegetatively, through layering. When branches are pushed down to moist ground by snow, they grow roots. Through such spreading, the isolated clumps of krummholz gradually expand outward into a continuous forest.

Traveling on southward I scurry beneath lowering snow clouds. Soon the trees stand in bogs and tilt every which way in "drunken forests," the scientific term for this phenomenon. Trees do not stay upright in bogs long, but tilt farther and farther until they topple over into the acidic water, very slowly returning to soil. Sphagnum peat bogs stretch for miles while the slim black lines of spruce run into them, ink lines on wet watercolor paper.

A true paradox of growth, this bog process is called paludification. At first this backward plant succession seems counterintuitive. Trees that have struggled for ten thousand years to form stunted forests then help create the very bogs that kill them. Tree roots need air, not acidic, poisonous water. Is this arboreal suicide?

Paludification begins in an impeded drainage, which forms a cast-iron skillet when the trees drop acidic needles. This acid then kills all plants except for peat moss. By bringing on their own demise, the spruce lay down the soil for their boreal descendants.

Podzolization, the process of building up podzol, which is Russian for a thin, infertile, ashlike soil, lays down yet another hard layer. I poke and examine it. No humus at all. The mattresses of sphagnum moss covering this layer hold clandestine ten-thousand-year atmospheric records: the Trinity bomb, the first atomic explosion in New Mexico, the bodies of animals, early hunters, children, and secrets. Eventually the bogs fill and become ground. A new generation of trees and a different, healthier forest begin.

A new raven teaches me to get down on my knees and poke

through the debris. Genuflection in humans is a good antidote for hubris. Kneeling, I discover a surreal land of starburst mossy stems ranging from bright red to orange to chartreuse to black. Monotony gives way to stunning beauty seen through a hand lens. Laid down so painstakingly for centuries, this, our North American bank account of life, has been collecting compound interest for the eon. Like wealthy playboys in Paris, we of the Lower Forty-Eight and Canadian provinces spend the soil's capital as if there were no tomorrow.

Seventeen jet-black ravens, painted with ink on golden cloth like seventeenth-century Japanese screens, flap through the blazing golds of dying larch needles. Soft starbursts of needles buzz yellow, backlit by the sun. Larch drop their needles to save energy in the winter, requiring a great deal of energy for new growth in late spring. The northernmost upright tree, the larch is a welcome contrast to the black toothiness of the spruce. It foreshadows the yellow quaking aspen leaves, which I will see if I make it out of here unfrozen.

Conifers have long enchanted man and bird alike; they sandwich broadleaf forests like latitudinal slices of bread, able to cope with the desiccation of the tundra and the extreme, dry heat of the desert. The needle-people exude a vegetative wisdom much older than the flowering plants.

By 5:15 it is night again. The raven settles in close to the trunk of a black spruce, and I beneath it in my pickup. Just two hundred miles south lies the end of this mud-sputtered existence.

Near us sleeps a pika in a den of frost-splintered rock softened with lichen, brier rose stems, and fireweed fluff. He nestles in the dry fibers of *Stereocaulan tomentosum*, the ubiquitous pioneer of terminal moraines and fire sites. This erect lichen is a beautiful silvery-gray, covered with toelike structures and reddish-brown disks of propagula. Across the Arctic and subarctic it covers bare gravel with soft cushions of miniature forests. Here, other lichen join it to offer a marvelous array of cups, dishes, curls, and cornucopias.

In the summer of 1991 fires raged in the interior of Alaska and Canada. As a result, many black spruce fell, their abundant cones popped open by the heat. With time, the released seeds will grow new trees. For now, the lichen with its algae component awaken each spring to fix nitrogen once again under the layer of burn. Cyanobacteria capture solar energy to combine water with carbon dioxide into organic molecules.

A new raven croaks up the dawn camouflaged against the burnt-out background. I do not remember where I parked to fall asleep in the early dark, but this morning I find myself inside an eery boreal holocaust. Unable to decompose in the dryness, burnt trunks lie indurate on an inhospitable soil. Their roots writhe upward like tangled hair. With the short growing season and harsh conditions, the tundra will not grow back any time soon: The caribou will not eat here for many, many years.

Then I watch the raven do something absolutely stunning. Its action is enticingly logical, yet amazing. I now understand what she has to do with the trees. She is caching seeds! Raven logic translated into forests.

Before I catch my breath from discovering such elegant symbiosis, the largest of the weasel family lumbers through my breakfast nook like an armored tank. Although wolverines are nasty fighters, this one seems nonthreatening. Just sort of ho-hum, "Morning, dear, where's my mug of coffee?" casual. A yellowed white streak bisects his fur, swerving up at his back end like a racing shoe swoosh. His demeanor today is definitely not indicative of this wolverine's speed.

Size is a striking feature of tundra animals: The giant deer, the moose; the largest weasel, the wolverine; and the great white and brown bears are built bulky to survive eighty degrees below zero. The larger the size, the smaller the percentage of surface area to volume, and the more heat preserved within. Immense size is the trade-off for the lack of diversity of life compared to the temperate forests.

As I travel down from Arctic toward the equator, I am finding ever more diverse ecosystems, and more biodiversity. Not only the number of species is increasing, but the number of families of species as well: Reptiles and amphibians are not found this far north. Through small adaptations to local conditions, entire families of animals find their position on this spinning ball of rock. The raven and I are two of the few species who spread ourselves all over the globe. Ravens survive well in the cold, see well in the dark, tolerate heat, and increase in number rapidly at the expense of other species.

In my camp the wolverine lumbers through the Labrador tea and reindeer lichen near my feet. I dare not move. Reindeer lichen, *Cladina rangiferina*, enchants me: pale, pale green one-quarter-inch-tall "aspen" trees crowding upward, only to be crushed beneath a newer layer of lichen. It becomes part of the bodies of not just caribou, but Inuits, Scandinavians, and many cultures around the pole. People in these cultures boil it, add it to pemmican, or mix it with berries. The Ojibwa boiled it and used it to bathe newborns. Technology has made the most ironic use of it: Highly sensitive to airborne, particulate pollution, it serves as an annual record of historic, worldwide conditions—our Arctic version of the miner's canary.

The tundra's blank photography paper is no longer developing merely in black and white. Undergrowth now stains the landscape vivid oranges, reds, and yellows: brilliant red bearberry, jet-black crowberry, rusty Labrador tea, golden cloudberry, and the subtle hues of lichens. In a Kodachrome of color, vascular plants now rise one or two feet above the ground, a huge shift from their previous dwarfed size and prostrate positions. The rusty reds of the heath family grow thick-leaved and flourish in the acid environment due to a special root fungus. The bell-shaped blooms of bog laurel seem to chime across the tundra.

Thirty-three miles south, curiously eroded twenty-five-foot-high mud formations rise above me like Hindu temple carvings. Composed of unconsolidated sea sediment, they weather into children's tops stacked on top of one another. Yellow cottonwood leaves on top of the snow suddenly stand up and pirouette in perfect synchronicity under the hand of an invisible choreographer.

Soon I come across blood-red creek water churning around bone-white stones. A giant must be dying upstream, or iron oxide is leaching out of freshly dug earth. A clue lies in the bulldozed dredges throughout the creek bottom, nothing left living. Someone has scraped out the guts of this wild stream. Mining is too hard to monitor up here; it appears that small operators may scrape off the tundra with impunity from environmental law.

To the south, trees stick up like ill-placed bottle brushes through fresh snow. For years, the Northwest Mounted Police passed through this area regularly on their annual seventeen-hundred-mile winter trek from Dawson City to Fort McPherson far in the frozen north. From 1904 on, each patrol spent two to three months checking residents and bringing mail all the way up to Herschel Island in the Beaufort Sea by dog team.

The snow begins in earnest, and I grow worried. The last barrier between me and the blacktop Dawson Highway, which leads to safety in British Columbia, is a formidable one: the Olgilvie Mountains.

My God, this is a primitive land! A bull elk bugles somewhere out there in the wind. Blizzard-laden cumulus clouds bombard one another like pool balls on the gray felt sky. In late September, by four o'clock, the Olgilvie Mountains swallow up most of that sky, day changes into night and fall into winter. Sixty miles before the end of the Dempster Highway, I see a serrated silhouette indicating a mountain range unhoned by ice. A dark forest clings tentatively to the mountainsides, rising to a very low timberline. Beneath the trees, rich minerals and petroleum.

Slipping tires on the icy north slope of the Olgilvie Mountains are a grim reminder: If the snow comes down harder before I reach the crest, I could be stuck.

On top of the serrated rock pass just before the road plunges down again, I pause to take one last long look at the tundra, the only landscape in North America relatively unchanged by human impact. Tundra zones on other continents have been heavily altered by grazing, tree felling, oil and mineral exploration. Here, where trees take centuries to grow, the wilderness is threatened by mining, drilling pads, construction sites, and the harvesting of the taiga for fiber.

Far below the sharp Olgilvie crest, two moose stand in the Klondike River. Seething silver water emerges from a crack high on a mountainside and disappears down off a high plateau. Snapping at me as I pass, the Olgilvies' northern side's night-maw lets me escape back into day through three-hundred-foot vulcanized rock teeth. Their sharp spikes stick up through the soft curving tundra mosses like teeth through the rubber prophylactic in the dentist's office.

Far below glints the Klondike River, which began the gold frenzy and its floods of prospectors opening up the wilderness a century ago. At this moment, with the sun directly in the cloud hole at the end of the valley, the Olgilvies bring a new sort of gold-seeker, whose treasure is mined in the heart.

At the Edge of Taiga

62° N, 133° W to
61° N, 133° W

*F*rom 64°40' north to 62° north, the season has spun backward, the gold trees re-leafing themselves. I have traveled backward through time. It is warmer; I am younger.

A reek of wood smoke permeates makeshift temples for the sacrifice of caribou and moose. The temple doors are infinitely wide and open to the rest of the world. Their ceilings are either of dark green canvas or of glittering, spinning gold leaves. Their walls stand elegantly ornamented with narrow columns of white, pink, and brown. The floors are of packed earth or crunching leaves. From cross poles hang the carcasses of caribou. All around are strewn the essentials of life—bicycles, buckets, fishing rods, items of clothing, toys, pots, cast-iron pans, cutting boards, axes lodged in tree stumps, stools and chairs, musical instruments, boats, ropes, books, a meat scale, a clock, floor mats, tarps, cots.

Not a soul around. I stand captivated by the lifestyle of the missing, but trusting, people who built these isolated hunting camps all along the gravel roads. I am enchanted with the camps, which include the whole family; an ideal, hands-on education, lessons in love, culture, and civil obedience. Perhaps this was my tribal family long ago in Europe. But here, it is Taska Indians.

Their obvious closeness to one another and the graciousness with which they live in the forest create a profound homesickness in me for something I have never known. I begin to long for that edge where the boreal forest ends and the temperate forest will embrace me, where there will be wood for central fireplaces, boards for homes, planks and masts for ships, fine-grained wood to vibrate with our classical music, and strong poles for our weapons. Just as the boreal woods are within the Taska, the temperate forest is part of my genes.

That bleeding, merging edge of true temperate forest is seventy miles to the south. Winter is coming.

Suddenly, unexpectedly, I find myself in Ross River Village. A gathering point for the Taska people, it is perched on the bank of a magical river. The birch tree leaves have turned the river's water yellow. In the remote, central Yukon Territories, Ross River Village is, today, a disarmingly lovely community of about five hundred white and Taska souls. Just eighty years ago Joseph Keele wrote this description of the then much smaller village:

> A small band of Indians, numbering about 110, including men, women and children, inhabit the country in the vicinity of the Ross and Pelly Rivers. These People trade their furs with Messrs Lewis and Field, who established a small trading post at the north … on the Liard River.[1]

In front of a large metal prefab warehouse, the native co-op, Taska people are loading huge boxes of vegetables into pickups with enthusiastic sled dogs in the back. Soon a long, icy winter will begin in this continental interior, and I wonder how wives and children will fill the long, dark hours. Then I remember the hunting camps where even young children help by gathering wood. Those who are not hunting dress out the carcasses and cook. Coming from a culture in which the young are isolated in cement boxes and abstract learning until they are eighteen, I am fascinated. Suddenly I understand the source of my loneliness.

Thirty ravens leap, hop, wrestle, preen, and flop on the banks of Ross River among the wind-stirred yellow leaves. They are making that

---

[1] Joseph, Keele *A Reconnaissance Across the Mackenzie Mountains on the Pelly, Ross, and Gravel Rivers* (Ottawa, Canada: Department of Mines, Government Printing Bureau), 11.

lovely waterfall sound they seem to gargle from the back of their throats. These birds are playing! They are asking, "What could I use this object for? What happens when I flip upside down in midair?" The raven treats everything as if it might have importance to his own life. Which, as a being like me who invents his own environment, is true.

In spite of the coming frost and black night, the big, bombastic birds enliven me. I take on the ravens' mood and am ecstatic in the bright fall weather. This is both good and bad. Good in that it lends me an elemental life force to proceed with my journey, and bad because it awakens my urge to explore. I want to drive north! To do so means crossing the swift Ross River channel on a fire-engine-red, one-car ferry and driving the 160 miles on the North Canol Road to its dead end at the border of the Yukon and Northwest territories. The Canol Road was built hurriedly during World War II to maintain a fuel pipeline to Whitehorse and beyond. South-southwest is the direction I need to go.

I stroll to the two-story Anglo store and buy one can of French Canadian beans (Harcourt Rouge), lunch meat, old packaged cheese, dried fruit, bottled water, aspirin, fuel, and matches. I stand in a queue, something I haven't done in months. Each of the Ross River folk in front of me must catch up on the vital information on which isolated life thrives. When it is my turn to pay for my goods, I have a moment of panic. I haven't enough Canadian cash left, and that is all the store accepts. I put back the expensive packages of meat and cheese and select some dreadful canned spaghetti. Then the bright-eyed clerk tells me about the Lower Canol Road.

"You shouldnah be headin' oot there sa late in the afternoon," she says in crisp, northern Canadian. "The temperature drops very quick at this time of fall and you could get yourself snowed in. Isn't nobody that goes down that way but once in a long while. You could get yr'self in trouble, girlie." I explain that I am completely equipped for survival for up to two weeks and that there are plenty of Taska people out hunting. I want her to ask what I'm doing up here, anyway. I want her to be curious about me, but she isn't.

The Lower Canol Road, a cliff-hanging product of homesick soldiers, begins well enough. By 4:20 P.M., just an hour after I set out, the road becomes uncompromising to a human driver's needs for the illusion of safety. Nowhere is the roadbed banked properly on curves. Each turn provides a dramatic revelation of the steep Pelley Mountains. One bend's view frames, far below, a gleaming silver river in late afternoon and, the strange black taiga trees clinging to the sides of precipitous mountains. The next bend exposes a steep, narrow valley of slate embedded with black coal lenses. Die Fledermazda's dark hood blends into those lenses, reminding me of my own carboniferous body. Another bend reveals a golden air mass crisply pouring down the mountain as dusk collects below. At 5:10 P.M. another twist reveals a muddy, tumultuous river bottom pocked with a zillion miniature lakes and bogs very good for moose.

On my left, the road bank of loose shale drops eight hundred feet to the river below. Stones are hitting my windshield from the loose sediment above. I am jostling about on the hard bench seat. The smell of damp clay gives me the willies. Filled with a hundred misshapened holes these rocks wheeze like Dmitri Schostakovich's orchestral flutes. Their conglomerate was laid down by a swiftly flowing river carrying heavy cobble mixed in with smaller gravel, a chaos of a river channel with greatly varying velocity. I close the window and turn on the heater.

I am driving through the Upper Lapie River Canyon, a formation that began when, eons ago, one-hundred-million year old horizontal layers of rock were buried several kilometers below the surface of the Earth. Plate tectonics ever so slowly folded the rocks through massive compression and strain. In several million more years, these rocks rose and tilted to their present position and were sliced open on the canyon wall. As if smooth and malleable as chocolate sauce and meringue, this metamorphosed schistose rock makes swirls that delight the eye.

The shoulders of the Pelly Mountains, each seeming to be the size of Rhode Island, are softened by mosses backlit by the slanting light into pink to red felts. A recent burn along the river bottom and up the canyon walls has left dead trunks standing stark against the rosy hues of the fireweed that is fixing nitrogen toward the forest's recovery. I half expect to see the trunks transforming into all the Taska men who have hunted over this territory for thousands of years. The thin soil will need decades to recover enough from the fire to protect a caribou herd again. Before the turn of the century, the fire cycle was very infrequent in central Yukon, and the caribou were able to alter their route around the smaller burns. Today the frequent man-made fires burn far and wide.

No dendritic lounge lizards need apply for this location. The Lapie River meanders tightly through the indurate trunks standing straight as soldiers, each with their spear of heat-cracked cones at the top. Nothing is easy, kind, or temperate about this forest yet. Nothing is softened, fat, or flush as in British Columbia or the Lower Forty-Eight. No fluid lines lull you to the life of abundance. Treetops weave no comforting canopy, but poke the sky with spikes split into two to four cone-laden spears, as if the whole vitality of the tree is in that upper tip. Often the trunks grow straight up a foot, take a right angle turn, go two feet horizontally, take another turn, and grow straight up again, memories of growing up crushed under obstacles. The taiga trees fall over frequently; their shallow root bases stick up like starched collars on stock-bound Puritans.

Even the aspen are not like the tall, graceful trees I grew up with in the Colorado Rockies. Instead, they are tortured, twisted souls. Many aspen trunks have crooks out to one side like Adam's apples. This is no longer the boreal forest but an interior taiga, all spiky and warlike against the hard lavender sky.

The flipside of being a receptive traveler is a tendency to adopt the character of one's surroundings. The black spruce I pass, burned and with their inner branches clustered up against their scraggly trunks, dismay me. When and if they sprout new growth, the tips will be intensely blue, like the blue spruce of Colorado. I feel all dark and prickly with slim hope of new growth.

Even the birds are few, big, dark, and loud. Spruce grouse, grungy gray with dishwater markings, waddle dumbly down the road in front of my tires, flashing a rusty tail rim as they evade the pickup's bumper. Safely in the branches of the spruce that line the road, they chortle at me as if they have cracked some obnoxious joke that I don't get.

Paying attention to the taiga changing is like watching myself age. Changes unfold so incrementally and subtly in the forest that it is hard for me to stay keen. To intensify my attentiveness I pretend that I am winding through the famous estate of the nineteenth century painter Frederick Church. Overlooking the Hudson River, Oleanna, the estate, was designed by the artist so that each turn of the road presented the traveler with a perfect composition for a Hudson River School painting. I round one corner and am struck by cone-shaped mountains rising straight upward to seven thousand feet. Around another corner, scrawny trees look like bristles studding a blackened fingernail brush. The fingernail brush goes on and on to the Arctic Circle. Around yet another corner, a lush scrim of poplar dance superimposed on the metallic river. At yet another curve, the icily distant Pelly Mountains speak of inaccessibility and vastness.

The Taska Indians never, while hunting, approach the headwaters of the Ross or Pelly Rivers. They believe evil spirits in the shape of giant Indians lurk there, around the Mackenzie Mountains' Continental Divide.[2] So my fears that kept me from driving north into the Mackenzies were not unfounded! In the Lower Forty-Eight, I can enter mountains at will at any point. It is not the same here. These boreal wilds offer no intimacy. They're cold, demanding.

At 61°47' north, I notice that the soil has begun to thicken to almost four inches in places, yet it still has no humus. The trees struggle along in it, tipping precariously off cliffs, out of the banks of the river, over boulders.

The pickup plunges beneath the bedrock's top level at the river crossings, its tires sending icy wings of spray to either side. Here, the

---

[2] *Ibid.*, 11.

ancient bedrock of the Continental Shield splits into feldspar trape-zoids but makes no soil to support the moss from which trees grow blithely upward. Is this a metaphor for a lack of life support or an af-fidavit for the incredible lightness of biological being? My choice.

In spite of the bone-numbing chill I feel, I begin to love this an-cient part of Canadian bedrock. Within this narrow, ice-free hallway running north-south between ice masses, older species were saved like rose petals in a book of days. Down the Beringian Corridor (the Bering Land Bridge across Alaska and down the central Yukon) wan-dered wooly mammoths, giant sloths, saber-toothed tigers, giant beavers, early bison and elk, with early man in close pursuit. This long, skinny refugium enabled the conifers and caribou to repopulate the forests relatively quickly when the ice receded from them.

Tourists flock to the jagged matterhorns of coastal Alaska and British Columbia, but it takes courage to travel these rounded moun-tains. I love interior Canada for its understatement, its treasure box of fauna clamped protectively between two rows of icy teeth. Little of the wild country between the Yukon and Mackenzie rivers was glaciated. The continental ice masses of the Pleistocene flowed down from the Alaska Range and the Canadian Coast Range but missed the Pelly Mountains. The Pelly and Ross rivers are young rivers that stag-ger through deposits of silt, mud, cobble, and the extensive ash of Mount Natazhat, which exploded 1,250 years ago.

A first-year bull moose stands in the center of the road, steam gust-ing from his nostrils. He is young enough not to know about hunters. Although I deeply respect the Taska people and their hunting way of life, I wish him a long life. Within fifty feet of him, I turn off my en-gine and headlights, drift to a stop, and sit motionless watching him for twenty-five minutes. He returns the honor, occasionally swinging his head slowly from side to side. He seems to be a loose hide bag of Lego-block bones glossed over with a healthy coat of gray to black fur, a ponderous English gentleman stepping out on a frigid London evening. Finally, he bows his head and sedately steps off the road, as if granting this strange lady her passage.

At one time the hunting pressure from both visiting whites and indigenous people was so great that the large game animals almost disappeared from this land. In 1910 Joseph Keele wrote that Indians with their newly acquired automatic weapons upon entering a herd would shoot until their guns were empty:

> Of late years, ... game of all kinds has become very scarce in some locations, owing to the extensive killing carried on by those who hunt for the market offered by mining camps. ... Head hunters who come into the country in search of fine specimens, do a great deal of damage, as they have been known after a day's hunting, to leave enough meat to spoil on a hillside to supply a prospector with provisions for a whole winter. These men at the end of their hunt will take out about twelve heads each, which would mean the killing of twenty animals (per one head taken).[3]

Yet even in the early 1900s a man with a gun could easily support himself. Mining camps of several thousand people sprang up overnight along the rivers. Men who failed at mining often turned to supplying others with food for their living, and the pressure on the animal populations greatly increased. Now I see very little game.

There is hope. The Canadian Fish and Wildlife biologists now cooperate with the Taskas to restore the balance. In the 1980s the Ross River Caribou Herd Project began with a count of the diminishing caribou herd and the initiation of a program to curtail the caribou's two main predators: wolf and man. Caribou numbers have since recovered beyond the wildlife managers' dreams, and wolves have been allowed to increase once more to cull the healthy caribou herd. By now, the wolves have recovered to their estimated original population.

When it becomes too dark to see, I park on a short side road along a roaring whitewater creek to sleep. It's twenty degrees below. Although my Qualifil bag has been rated by the good folk of L. L. Bean to forty below, I wish the CEO was in the bag with me. All night long, the stream thunders and the wind howls. All of my water bottles

---

[3] *Ibid.*, 24–30.

freeze. In the black of night, I do not realize that I am balanced on the Continental Divide under Fox Mountain at seventy-five hundred feet, the highest peak in the area from which waters flow north to the Arctic or west to the Pacific Ocean.

At 5:00 A.M., a very eerie world of beginnings. I awake in a war zone— a pitted landscape, poorly drained, and covered with little black lakes. Each of the round, ice-melt lakes has mist rising off its surface. All the grass blades are glass spindles, the only objects picking up light from the unborn sun. I leap into my truck seat hoping to warm up as I drive, but at ten degrees below zero, the little engine has no intention of sharing its heat. I keep going.

Fifty-nine miles below Ross River, other trees creep in: white spruce, lodgepole pine, more aspen.

Slowly, slowly, the black night is illuminated with crusts of bright edges, and those edges slowly glue themselves into silhouettes, and those silhouettes slowly hint of chiaroscuro, and those chiaroscuros expand into volumes. The world is rising up out of the underworld. Demeter is giddy.

The white spruce, tall and healthy, begin to crowd together with their blue-tipped new growth and Christmas-tree shapes. Bunches of golden gypsy mushrooms, caps as big as saucers, impersonate parasols. Driving southward, I feel as though I have earned this southern boreal forest thick with needles, lush in branches, and robust in canopy. Soon a long, calm lake is flickering between the spruce trunks like a stroboscope. I drive more quickly: The road has transformed from muck to bright, dry gravel; the lake flickers faster.

A temperate zone forest, the very first of it! It has pulled itself up out of that pitted and scarred landscape, straight out of the rubble with little benefit of soil. Before me, a full, lush lodgepole forest grows on the banks of the aptly named Quiet Lake. I am smelling home.

The Icy Edge

61° N, 135° W

F jords! I love to sit in a kayak and gaze crooked-necked, up eight hundred feet of graywacke rock wall to a blue glacier pouring in extremely slow motion out of a V in the ridgeline. Nothing defines North America's western edge above the Hoh River as much as the fjord; British Columbia has some of the finest in the world. A fjord, a Norwegian word meaning "bay," is a long, narrow arm of sea that occupies a deep U-shaped valley carved out by a glacier. Its near-vertical walls are periodically broken by glacier or stream channels, called hanging valleys, high above sea level. Hanging valleys are left suspended when the main glacier cut an existing stream valley quickly down toward sea level.

After a winter hiatus in the Lower Forty-Eight, anticipation propels me during the two days' drive from Seattle toward Quiet Lake in the high interior of the Yukon. However, at the north end of the Cassiar Highway, I am moved to turn west toward Atlin Lake, located an enticing seventy miles from the coast of Inside Passage. This area, where the Yukon, British Columbia, and Southeast Alaska converge, is one of the most geologically tumultuous areas on the planet. Its geography was shaped by the Pacific Ocean Plate, which swept northward from South America picking up fragments of southern California and continuing on toward Alaska. As it sideswiped North America in British Columbia, it piled up fragments of land, older islands, continental shelves, and basalt flows from the ocean floor into coastal mountains. The mountainous coastal landmass was then hacked apart by water and ice into the Alexander Archipelago.

The coastal mountains were pushed up so high that they formed an impenetrable barrier to weather and people. This wild segment of the globe—which includes Glacier and Yakitat bays, the Wrangell–St. Elias and Kluane mountain ranges, and the Tatshenshini-Alsek Wild and Scenic River system—has been recognized by the United Nations as a global treasure.

The Wrangellian landmass continues southward through British Columbia's Coastal Range to the forty-ninth parallel (no political overtones here). One of its peaks, Mount St. Elias, which rises from near sea level to 14,163 feet, achieves more relief from its base to its summit than does 29,000-foot Mount Everest. This wild mélange of mountains stymied human migration except for small groups of Tlingit ancestors, people of amazing physical stamina and technical know-how. The rise of sea level due to glacial melting during the last ten thousand years drowned the oldest settlements under four hundred feet of water. Arriving by sea, according to recent anthropological conjecture, the first people did not travel up the dangerous rapids above the fjords, where formidable whitewater rivers tumble from 10,000-foot peaks to sea level in 50 to 150 miles.

The most recent descendants of the original inhabitants, the Tlingits, have done what their ancestors did not in creating routes up Taku Fjord and the Chilcoot Pass, the only viable passageways from the Inside Passage to Canada's high, dry interior. Until recently there were no roads through this terrain. Now, a squiggly little road from the Alcan Highway parallels the Chilcoot Trail from the interior to deadend at Skagway, Alaska.

Longing to understand firsthand how a mountain creek transforms itself into Taku Fjord's ice-littered shores, I hoist on a pack and attempt to plunge southwest from Atlin Lake along a peat-mired trail to reach the Taku River. As I tramp through deeper and deeper bogs, the black flies attacking my ears, I realize that even the most experienced packers would have trouble following this indistinct trail. Before turning back in defeat, I encounter two trappers, each loaded with a one-hundred-pound pack of hides, heaving in from farther south near Telegraph Creek. They are completely exhausted and cannot even speak with me. Instead, they skirt around me as if I were a wild animal with an undesirable hide. At least they add dignity to my failure, informing me that this trail had beaten up the toughest of mountain men.

Even if I could have found my way seventeen miles over bogs and ridges to the Taku River, I lacked a dugout canoe, the whitewater skills, and the technical genius of the Taku Band of Inland Tlingit to run the Taku River all the way down to Lynn Canal.

Turning back, I imagine the Taku Glacier pouring down from the ice fields to enter Taku Fjord, which I saw when I journeyed up from Lynn Canal the year I worked in Juneau, Alaska. The Taku Fjord slices inland for more than a hundred miles into northern British Columbia's high arctic desert on the far side of the coastal mountains. Its canyon runs more than one thousand feet deep.

In the village of Atlin, I buy food and camp stove fuel and head up into the mountains to the east. Following one of the many mining roads that squirrel all over these hills, I climb from the river valley bottom nine hundred feet straight up a mountainside until huge granite talus stymies my progress.

What a magnificent place to sleep! I watch the sun plummet below the ice field and the glaciers fifty miles west of my camping spot as I build a fire and cook my dinner. All night long, I keep glancing at the two ominously dark mining tunnel entrances in front of me in the side of the mountain. I don't believe in ghosts, but one never knows about these miners. Those who chase illusive dreams may still wander.

The next morning the sun drills into my skull around four o'clock; early June days are nineteen hours long.

After a quick breakfast of bread, cheese, and coffee, I scramble for an hour up the last seven hundred feet. It takes the gyrfalcon just seven minutes and one thermal to travel this distance. Perching high above Atlin Lake in the northwest corner of British Columbia, I gaze westward toward a huge ice field. At 4,640 feet above sea level, I huddle in the black and white tundra brushed with sepia washes, hiding from the bone-chilling wind among low, leafless willow and berry shrubs. The air is witheringly dry. Small flies, sounding like a hundred tiny lawn mowers, sting me relentlessly just above the ears and along the hairline.

Behind me, to the east, looms the Coast Range, appearing like the huge barrier that it actually is—geologically, meteorologically, anthropologically, and theologically. Mountain behind mountain continues forever. Two thousand feet below, flat-bottomed, U-shaped valleys are threaded by macraméd rivers.

I face west. Atlin Lake gleams like polished silver as far north and south as I can see. It is just one of the many fjord lakes between my perch and Lynn Canal in Southeast Alaska. Above the lake, glaciers sweep from 2,190 feet at the water surface to 7,000 feet in a mere seven miles like white, ethereal curtains.

Beyond the lake to the west rises an immense earth-warp, trailless and impenetrable except to ice climbers and helicopters. In these mountains, airborne Pacific Ocean shudders, stalls, and dumps its load on the Llewelyn Icefield and Glacier. Just a short hop over Mount Nesselrode, Juneau's computers whir in the voracious, political heart of Alaska.

In my mind, I rise on hawk wings to sail over the ice field to the bergshrund, the crevasse that marks the beginning of Taku Glacier. A glacier is the vibrant beast of Pacific storms that has swallowed the sun's energy and the ocean's energy and transformed them into ice-rock. It melts itself away at its bottom as it gathers itself in above; it is a link from the high, dry British Columbian interior to the sloshing channels of the Pacific.

All muggy, swarthy, unkempt clouds. From the Llewelyn Icefield, this ice-snake pours itself down the mountainside glowing lighter than anything else in the landscape. House-sized crevasses curve concentrically downward, crossing the glacier in graceful scallops. Thunderous, low frequency explosions emanate from deep within the glacier.

Taku Glacier is deep blue under dark clouds. Its powdery turquoise deepens to cobalt inside the jagged seracs, the three-hundred-foot ice teeth that jut upward from the grid of ice crevasses. Subterranean rivers bellow beneath the glacier, disgorging its interior, cutting channels inside the ice with their swift volumes of water. When glaciers melt, such rivers deposit unsorted rock and dirt ground by ice in the form of fat eskers on the flat valley bottoms. An esker can be a hundred feet high and run for miles in curves like a snake.

When the river roars out from under the glacier's terminus, its water is dirty brown and is intimidating with thunder. If icebergs discharge into the river, they will resculpt themselves continuously, rolling in the murky water in front of the undercut, three-hundred-foot-high ice wall. The puissance of water can gut a glacier.

The fjord walls shoot straight up to precariously balanced talus, ranging from one foot to fifty feet in diameter, hundreds of feet above. The glacier plucks such talus from the bedrock, embeds it within its sides, and chisels the terrain into new shapes. These shapes will later sculpt future forests, determining which trees grow where.

At the ice edge, I clamber through Sitka alder shrubs that pluck the land right out from under the glacier with the power of root. On moraines so steep, so loose, so impermanent, and so treacherous that humans can be buried, the willow roots serve as rebar to reinforce the loose stone.

Days later, as I float quietly in a kayak on water the color of dark iron and opaque with glacial flour, I scrutinize the glacier's discharge cave from the distance of a quarter mile. An evocative tunnel, formed of ice arches in layers of greater and greater constriction, from sky blue to dark night blue, it penetrates deep into the glacier. It would be deadly to follow it inward. Its inner walls are carved in conchoidal fractures that, at one moment, gleam like diamond facets, and the next, disappear as the ice crashes into the mirror-still water to create tsunamis that roll out toward unwary kayakers. Calving glaciers can be deadly.

Awe is evoked from this river of ice, its beauty, its immensity, the blue of the mineral, ice. It is not a blue of this Earth. It is an ethereal lapis lazuli, a cerulean thunder.

Ice has a quality of capturing sunlight, siphoning it into long strands that it stretches in taut molecular silks. In granular surfaces, it transfixes light in hexagonal brocades until pressure bears down from the ice above.

Ice vibrates in a fourth form of light physics different than refraction, reflection, and absorption. Something angelic. Something transcendent.

Humans attempt to bring back images, but photography cannot capture the immensity and danger of glaciers. Photographs do not hold within them the Earth-shaking crashes that vibrate the ground or the cold dampness that permeates the atmosphere. Images cannot re-create those difficult nights of survival, sleeping on the ice-cold stone near a glacier that calves all night long. A color slide does not revolve with the kinetic grace of a four-ton berg as it rolls ominously in the ice-gray channel.

My kayak floats down the fjord toward the Inside Passage. Seven hundred feet above my head, hanging glaciers poke straight down out of the clouds, sharp, symmetrical blades of ice. Their hard blue ice has hung there forever, yet it seems that all that volume should have fallen long ago. The tops of these hanging glaciers disappear into the clouds.

Plummeting through the thick fog of the Coast Range by truck, on foot, or by kayak, I have the sensation of diving that I had as a child. Slicing into the water of the swimming pool from the hot concrete or into a fern-lined plunge pool—that sensation of bubbles vibrating past my cheeks, past my neck, down my shoulders, swirling under my arms, around my torso, down past my thighs, and following my feet in a tickling column of trailing bubbles. Descending to the coast from the dry interior is like opening my eyes underwater to discover ferns and epiphytes in a green swirl around my head. I've been swallowed by an airborne ocean or an earth-bound cloud.

When I would dive as a child, I would raise my arms over my head and press my hands back-to-back in an inside-out-prayer. Now, as I catch glimpses of these fog-shrouded white spruce, they are doing just that—pointing their bodies like hands to dive into the mist.

Their needles are exquisitely designed to pluck water right from the air onto a highly maximized surface area so that it slides down their skins, down their twigs, down their branches, down their spines, into the web of their roots. With millions of needles per tree, the surface area which contacts the fog can collect forty inches of water per year, in addition to the moisture the needles collect from snow or rain.

The first trees to appear out from under the retreating Taku ice are catching water every hour and day that the air holds moisture— which is most days. Clearcutting, an artificial edge, shifts the climate toward drought because there are no trees to capture the volumes of water from fog with their needles. I have hiked through brutal clearcuts in the Gifford Pinchot National Forest of wet, southwest Washington to find the ground under a clearcut as dry as bone.

The black cottonwoods in fall, if they had eyes to open in the midst of these dark conifer forests, would see their own leaves as golden bubbles slung in spiral galaxies all around their black axes.

Paddling Down the Fjord Toward Lynn Canal: A Seal's Perspective

An unearthly corporeality. These waters are as uncanny and insubstantial as landing on Mars.

In the long, narrow fjord, my kayak rides so low in the steely water that my eyes float just inches above the surface. From a seal's perspective I watch waves slip outward toward the bare rock mountains that rise straight up from great depths. Frigid fog shrouds their upper slopes, which, from my perspective, do not exist. Each paddle blade cleaves the gray plane, pushing it back three feet, and rises noiselessly. I twist the paddle swiftly near the stroke's end just as it slips from the surface. Icy water thick as molasses slides off to rejoin its own skin. Noiselessly. Left blade, right blade, noiselessly. Pushing water back into a murmuring swirl, my paddle withdraws smoothly, like silk, from a ghostly eddy. I am not floating on a fjord, but am submerged in it.

No vision compares to this in all of the Lower Forty-Eight. Towering rock faces rise up in monstrous, faceted walls. High above, notched and spired stairs are crammed in the deep cracks where talus has fallen. I float along the rock walls' perpendicular joint with the sea, an organic fleck in a dead land. This stone is less than fifty years uncovered by ice. Peering up the rock gaps for brown bears, I scrutinize the land with the mind and eyes of a seal surfacing to breathe—curious, bright-eyed, dog-muzzled, sharp to the scent of danger.

Balanced in an eye slit of fiberglass, I watch ice sculptures float stealthily by. Cold, primordial sculptures, they are constantly melting into sharp-finned, layered depositions tilting at all angles like sinking ocean liners. Hooks, anvils, sails, gull wings float by. Angular and unforgiving, they bely their deep substance under the surface. Kayakers should not approach within two hundred feet at any time; icebergs can roll and take a kayak with them.

Ancient, the bergs fizzle out compressed atmosphere that the snow swallowed hundreds of years ago. Dust and ash from old volcanoes sink slowly to the bottom. As I watch the icebergs float by, I feel the throb of discovery that John Muir felt as he explored Glacier Bay and then broadcast through his beautiful prose to the rest of the world.

Under the surface, dark forms follow my kayak and the others on the river. With curiosity characteristic of higher predators, the porpoise and orcas follow, vastly inquisitive about these strange whales that swim on top of the water. I worry that they might accidentally flip me, yet I love the power of their black bulks and having their deep water souls close by.

Kittiwakes swirl down to the water surface to pluck up the rising brine shrimp, which die of shock when they meet the clear water of glacial discharge. Rising in a spiral of breaking-glass cries, these brilliant white gulls glint sharply in the sun.

Phalaropes bank in perfect unison, transposing from white to rust-red and back. Four hundred bird bodies precisely pivot white, red white, red white, red every three seconds, carving the air by an internal rhythm and the logic of the wind. In shallows, they land and spin and spin and spin, shining like toy tops, stirring up organisms from the bottom. Rufous with white collars edged in dark brown, they are lovely, shining, spinning feathered nodules of pure bird energy.

Dark, strange liquid churns about the rocky points of land that jut aggressively into the strong tidal currents and frighten me. I escape around one into a bay with its glowing glacier terminus. Turquoise eddies swirl out from my paddle like speculations. At the very top edge of the glacier, chiseled nunataks, or rock peaks, protrude straight up into the clouds, as if they are fingers grasping the sky, desperate not to be swept out to sea.

Eighty feet of ice starts falling in a column; its shrouded sound reaches my ears like a muffled explosion. The whole world is turned upside down. Brine shrimp rise from the nonsaline bottom to die in saline shock, sacrificed for the black-legged kittiwakes swirling out of the glass sky like swollen flakes of snow. Layers upon layers of their cries create a soundscape so cacophonous, so wondrous, so creaking, that it uncoils a spiral universe. The beginning of time must have sounded like these kittiwakes.

The aftershock wave mounds toward my kayak from a half mile away. I am dressed warmly, but not in a dry suit; if I am flipped, there is a technique by which I can reenter the kayak, but I don't want to try it out here. I turn to face the wave, a small glass splinter before an immense steel wall. Heart bruising, neck pulsing, the kayak slides up the wall and then tips sharply into the sky.

All there is is sky—and the kayak flying toward it.

As I tip downward, I nose into the viscous gray-green underworld of whales. On the next wave, I tilt up, then down, until the kayak rocks gently again.

I paddle into a shallow bay where I can walk out if I flip and skirt a little closer to the glacier. Still, it would be life threatening to submerge: no shrubs, no wood, no fire. I am dressed warmly in layers of wool and synthetic fleece, and in the boat in waterproof bags are two more changes of clothes and a butane stove. Still, I am frightened.

In the turquoise mirror my image floats upside down against the glacier face. Two hundred feet above me, turquoise pillars, icy cary-atids, hold the weight of centuries on their white marble shoulders. Their images also reverse and penetrate the water upside down. My paddle pokes into one and stirs her into turquoise spirals.

After noon, thick clouds wallow in on their bellies. No sun slices through. Viscous, muggy, ill-kept mist, gray moans of water, inscrutable bays. It is low tide; the hieroglyphics of snowfields descend to speak with the hieroglyphics of the mud flats that stretch for miles from the glaciers' discharge.

It feels as if I am floating four billion years ago as the Earth was first dreaming of life. Time speeds up. The first green slime crawls up the stone. I cannot breathe this atmosphere: The plants have yet to increase the oxygen. Cellular life is inventing itself under my nose. It is time to get out of the boat and camp.

It is twilight, and I hurriedly cook and eat a freeze-dried meal, glancing around constantly for bears. It is only twenty-seven degrees Fahrenheit at 4:30. I quickly stuff all items that smell, including toothpaste, in a round metal canister, bury it under a heavy rock, and in the kayak skedaddle across the quarter-mile-wide bay to sleep. Although the new location does not guarantee there will be no bears, at least it does not add my food smells to my odoriferous body.

I sleep very fitfully, dreaming of hurtling through the bowels of a glacier in a river.

The following morning I creak on cold bones down to a rock on the shore, which hides half of my body when I squat. Scientists have found that the tides are the best way to dispose of human waste in a land of little vegetation. Without brushing my teeth, I strike the tent, loosely load the kayak, and paddle the quarter mile back across the bay. Frantically, I search for the metal food canister that I have lost under the nondescript talus. Finally—toothpaste, then coffee, then those powdery eggs with specks of red and green that mix up in lumps. After breakfast, I briefly explore.

Climbing up a seven-foot block of transparent blue ice, I lie on my side and, by pressing my legs together, feet apart, and barking, pretend to be a seal. I climb down, drag my kayak toward the icy water, climb in, and, securing my spray skirt, shove off to skulk along great faces of stone under cascades of water. Waterfalls here are like no waterfalls I have ever seen below; the North Cascades have the general gist, but they do not have the volume. These waterfalls are persistent, pulsing. Shooting outward at right angles to the stone, they arch back to earth with a powerful grace.

A giant has scraped the sides of these mountains with comb teeth one hundred feet apart so that silver waterfalls shoot the guts of the sky down in evenly spaced, vertical lines. The effect in the distance is of glowing lightning frozen on the face of dark gray rock wall.

This is not a gentle beauty, but a beauty lined with terror and bare rock. It devours my old way of seeing, kayak and all. A killing, slicing, chilling, deepening, stone-toothed beauty opens an insurgent way of seeing. It gouges me out a U-shaped soul.

Part Two

❧

The Coast of BC:
Home of the
Old Growth Rain Forest

Introduction

56°40' N, 130° W to
50°45' N, 127° W

On a map, the wild western edge of British Columbia looks like an angular version of Ed Abbey's labyrinthine desert canyons and mesas drowned in a bright blue ocean. This relatively new slice of geography, which continues to be cut by fire and ice (vulcanism and glaciation) and air (the ever-churning cyclones of weather), stretches from Alaska to below the forty-ninth parallel. Victoria, Vancouver Island, lies south of the San Juan Islands, Washington.

This wild edge is not a straight coast, as between San Diego and Del Mar, but a coastline so cut and convoluted with fjords, channels, inlets, islands, rapids, and arms that the north-to-south distance must be multiplied by a factor of one hundred or more to estimate the actual mileage of the shoreline.

The value of British Columbia's wild coast is clearly apparent when viewed in contrast to the coastlines of Oregon, California, and the bottom third of Washington, which have been chopped, sold, and developed. The professed "wilderness" of the Olympic National Seashore is encroached upon by clearcuts, in some places less than a fifth of a mile back from the shore. Forests along the seaward edge of British Columbia have had between ten thousand (at the north) and thirteen thousand years to develop since the last Ice Age.

Extremely few North Americans have encountered this portion of their own continent, an edge relatively untouched, so that the breathing of its massive forests powers a healthy atmosphere and their detritus feed a healthy marine life system. It is a land that hints at the magnificence of unaltered ecosystems.

For years I longed to explore this truly wild edge firsthand, and in 1992, I got my wish. I joined five Canadians on a sailboat to run one of the wildest coastlines left on Earth. Peter, our leader, had masterminded, planned, and funded the trip. Captains Cindy and Baden had built and owned the beautiful sailboat we used, the *Sinbad*. Ian and Karen, a couple in their early twenties who worked replanting the clearcuts of British Columbia for the government, were energetic environmentalists. Ian was trip photographer and Karen was cook. Peter and Ian were father and son.

Despite the idealistic goal of our journey, to map the current state of the Ancient Forest along mid-coast British Columbia, tension mounted among the crew. Peter had cut the trip short by a month in order to hurry back to the environmental politics of Victoria, the province's capital. Ironically, the required speed of our trip would now hamper, if not destroy, the opportunity for good work by the writers, photographers, and natural historians in the crew. Identifying, mapping, photographing, drawing, and writing about strange, new plants simply will not be hurried.

From the Yosemite-like fjordland north of Bella Bella to the northern tip of Vancouver Island, this world of rough seas and deep fjords is relatively untrammeled. Because immense tidal variations confined in very narrow channels create standing waves that rival Grand Canyon rapids, powerful boats are needed to navigate the fjords. By tuning our timing to the tides, we were able to use a combination of sailboat and Zodiac inflatable motorized boats to penetrate these secret waterways.

The wilderness is quite wide along British Columbia's coast, extending from submerged canyons and plateaus eastward to the crest of the Coast Range, 200 to 350 miles across. On a global map of the world's wetlands, other coastal regions are longer, but Canada's west coast has the greatest breadth due to the multiple waterways of the Hecate Lowlands and the deep fjord penetration into the mountains. This coastline holds the most massive forests of North America, and compared to the forests of the Lower Forty-Eight, they are far, far more intact. Even the remarkable rain forest of the Tongass National Forest in Southeast Alaska was severely clearcut following our government's agreement with Japanese pulp mills after World War II, which granted the mills unlimited wood for fifty years. Those contracts have recently been withdrawn.

Canadian fisheries once ranked among the top ten fisheries on the globe, employing 130,000 people and earning $416 million. Washingtonian, Alaskan, and Canadian fisheries greatly depend on the health of Canadian forests and waters, although Alaskans refuse to acknowledge such interdependency. As of the late 1980s, the salmon and other fisheries in both countries have taken a nosedive due to overfishing, timber stripping, siltification, river damming, ocean warming, and humanity's denial of the interconnectedness of all living systems.

One half of all the world's fresh water originates in Canada. An unbelievable torrent of fresh water pours down ten thousand feet from the ice fields and glaciers of the Cordilleran highlands, joined by the two hundred plus inches of annual rainfall from the Pacific storm-bucket brigade. This fresh water is key to wetland and marineland health in its control of the salinity in the Hecate Lowlands and represents half of the major driving pulleys of the immense chaos machine that drives the Pacific Coast and atmospheric life forces. It is humbling to remember that in Puget Sound, we not only benefit from but we *are* the Fraser River's bioregion. The Fraser's gravity machine drains a much larger land and forest area than, for instance, the Columbia River does, the latter now dammed and relatively becalmed.

We came on this journey to watch a forest being born again on bedrock, to understand how the glaciers covered the distance from high mountain to the ocean, to watch the fjords drop in steps from hanging glaciers into deep glacial lakes, waterfalls, rapids, inlets, and ocean channels. The five Canadians and I desired access into the deep fjords shrouded in mist that cut far inland at east-northeastwardly angles from the coast. We longed to penetrate these jagged cracks in the Earth's crust that were ground into U-shaped canyons by ice. We wanted to record the organic feast that existed there—its mass, diversity, complexity—as a rare example of what life was like before extraction industries altered this continent forever.

In 1992, at the time of our travels, much of the Ancient Rain Forest was slated to be cut within the next decade. Since then, the massive efforts of thousands of Canadian, European, and American citizens have slowed the cutting. New forestry guidelines and some enforcement have lessened the damage of clearcutting. The timber giant MacMillan Bloedel has quit clearcutting altogether in Canada due to impressive grass-roots economic pressure from Europeans.

Unlike the states of the Lower Forty-Eight, for which detailed forest maps are available, satellite images were the only guide available for British Columbia. The region's outdated topographical maps could not represent what was forest and what was clearcut. To "ground truth" a satellite image means to walk, ride, climb, and float every foot of ground possible, drawing in the actual clearcut, building sites, and roading that are currently in place. Our task—to ground truth the satellite images of British Columbia's coastline and, thus, redraw the woefully erroneous maps of the Forest Service to determine what was left of the original rain forest—would be basically impossible.

But we'd have a hell of a time trying.

The Land of Origin

52°08' N, 128°05' W

Old Bella Bella

The intoxicating stench of wet earth and wood rises upward around me as I walk through Old Bella Bella. Every one of its several hundred citizens seems to be out on its muddy dirt roads today, strolling to the wooden church, going to meetings, heading toward the fishing fleet, pushing strollers, and generally appreciating the seldom-seen sun. They all greet me with nods or wide grins, acknowledging the unusual presence of a stranger in their midst. A third of them are carrying large serving pots toward the church—this must be a day of community. I smile. These potlucks remind me of the immense potlatches, or giving ceremonies, the native Canadians used to honor a wedding, a chief, the raising of a totem pole, or other important life events. Various tribes would travel hundreds of miles to receive elaborate gifts and partake in the feast, which gave credence to the person, family, or village of distant neighbors.

Back in the present, the pots, giving off the aromas of meats and cheeses, fill me with desire to live here, perhaps to teach, to winter it through, to make friends, to join clubs, to cook my special cheesecake for other potlucks, to join the church, to be welcomed into a family, to immerse my alien ears in the lovely lilt of the Heiltsuk language, to eat as they eat, to learn to crew a small fishing vessel, and to mesh my own rhythms with the rhythms of sea storm and swarming fish.

Because the Heiltsuk have long been a nation closely tied to the sea, the men and their sons still spend most of their lives on the Inside

Passage. The majority of the Heiltsuk people now live clustered around government facilities in new Bella Bella, the larger village on a separate island from Old Bella Bella.

Old Bella Bella, a fishing village hovering at the edge of rain forest and pounding sea, has probably been here in one form or another since the great skirts of ice retracted from the central British Columbia Coast. Although they lived in an unusually rich coastal biotic zone before Bella Bella existed, these forest- and sea-dependent people originally spread themselves out in small bands and family groupings throughout the region, lessening their impact on the resources in one area. The mild winters, moderate summers, two hundred inches of annual rainfall in some locations and more than one hundred inches in most, offered a life relatively assured of food. Abundant shellfish and game, salmon "so thick you could walk on their backs," and berry bushes allowed much time to invest in ceremony, potlatches, storytelling, visiting from tribe to tribe, and the creation of lavish works of art.[1] According to comparative studies in anthropology, time is not the sole factor in the creation of a rich culture. The coastal tribes were simply a remarkably inventive and creative people. Being a wordsmith myself, I believe that their complexity and subtlety of language contributed as much to their creativity as did the food abundance.

Old Bella Bella seems to have inflated overnight with prefab buildings: two schools, the Royal Canadian Mounted Police Headquarters, an aluminum town hall, government office trailers, and a large Wakiway Community Hall. We gas up the Sinbad and gather supplies. We are about to penetrate a mythic land—the fjord that is the center of the Heiltsuk story of origin. I ache with anticipation.

---

[1] Susanne F. Hilton, "Haishais, Bella Bella and Oowekeeno," in *Handbook of North American Indians,* Vol. 7, *Northwest Coast* (Smithsonian: Washington, D.C., 1990), 777.

The Ellerslie Watershed

52°35' N, 125°55' W

We sail north out of Old Bella Bella through a series of choppy channels, Heiltsuk ancestral territory. My overactive imagination populates the mist-laden shores with tiny villages, some so small they consist of only one extended family, each having its own chief—Chief Kyete, Chief Boston, Chief Wacash. It is to Chief Kyete's homeland we now sail. He resided at the entrance to Spiller Channel, and the Ellerslie, our next destination, takes off from the east side of the mouth of Spiller Inlet. Each family chose for its home the shores of an isolated fjord or upper lake in the glacial channels that stretched inland toward the ten-thousand-foot Coast Range peaks. The families' language and customs would have diverged over the millennia if it had not been for frequent potlatches, the periodic giving feasts that tied the ocean-going people together.

As of 1905, whites still saw the ruins of these villages peak from the forest. Most of the Heiltsuk who had survived the epidemics of white man's diseases had already gathered to live around the trade center and services of Fort McLoughlin of the Hudson Bay Company. Having read the tantalizing accounts of the villages by one early employee of Hudson Bay, stationed there in 1833–1834, I am overwhelmed with anticipation.

Dr. Tolmie, who referred to the people as Bil-Billa or Haeeltzuk, took a boat around to these small communities on November 27 and 28, 1834. Because many of the Heiltsuk were against the intrusion of whites, he was heavily guarded as he made his way back to each chief's house. He wrote that he was treated to "conjuring entertainment and dance" and a grand feast and was shown a fine leather belt decorated with three rows of thimbles given to a chief by Captain Vancouver, probably in 1793.[2]

---

[2] Captain John T. Walbran, *British Columbia Coast Names, 1592–1906*, originally printed in 1906, reprint and update, The Library Press (Vancouver, B.C.: 1971), 46.

Captain Vancouver and Dr. Tolmie are long gone, but we have Captain Baden, who now spreads out marine charts and maps. The coastline is beautifully intricate, with many inlets, passageways, and land squiggles. When I ask how much of this territory has been surveyed biologically, the Canadians reply that no biological surveys whatsoever have been completed along this wild edge. The traditional knowledge of the plants and animals, the Heiltsuk science, dies with each Heiltsuk lifestyle shift.

We find that the governmental topographical maps do not match the actual landforms. It is one thing to glance at a landscape from afar and another to use maps to actually put your feet on it. Inaccuracies have a way of telescoping into hours of misery on the ground. We have come armed with Forest Service maps, aerial photographs, and topos to find discrepancies between what actually exists and the forest industries' distortions and to match ground surveys with satellite images.

Up here, miles from white men's towns, "no population" equals no government veracity. Nonwhites are dispensable, Injuns don't count. This is changing, and we intend to speed up this change.

Of the fifty-four major watersheds of over sixty-four thousand acres left on this coast, only six were still uncut. Several of these were slated to be roaded the winter after our journey and cut soon thereafter. Because there was no resistant and vocal population base, the Forest Service was encouraging an irreversible leveling of irreplaceable ecosystems by an unregulated industry. Our trip was for the express purpose of recording this wild, intact ecosystem for humanity before it was gone forever.

To reach the Ellerslie, we must sail north from Bella Bella up into Johnston Channel, up Dean Channel, and up through Fisher Channel through confusing, interwoven fjords.

We propel slowly through the fog soup as if it were made of white beans and ham hocks. The marine charts are like Renaissance paintings—each character, each nuance has a meaning. In a rococo pattern, bright yellow jigsaw pieces of ill-fitting peninsulas and islands are interlaced with deep turquoise fjords. The Heiltsuk place names crackle as if with electricity: *Klekane, Khutze, Aaltanhasa, Kxngeal, Kiskiata, Kiskosh, Kitdal.* No Anglo names up here. No Anglos, either.

Steep humps of dark mountains emerge from the ghostly fog, their distant tops sliced off by clouds. Up their sides, snakes of mist reveal and submerge the vertical forests that enfold us as if we are roiling in the ocean depths. Cliffs of white granite mottled with black lichen occasionally slice through the trees. This is continental bedrock, scraped and hacked off in truncated spurs by the ice. Never have I experienced such a vertiginous landscape.

I am in awe of the trees before me, which took ten thousand years to gain their tenacious hold on the steep sea edge.[3] The dusky greens of western red cedar, hemlock, and Sitka spruce are slashed by the vibrant chartreuse of alder and the golds of vine maple that take hold in the V-shaped avalanche chutes.

I am struck by the immense ability of these forests to retain moisture. The mist, heavy as a burlap shroud, catches on the tree canopy, coating each needle with a pillowcase of water. Enough moisture to water a city is captured by every two mountains. In contrast, each brown, scoured clearcut we pass is much drier and is as bare as if the skin of the planet had been scraped down to cartilage. Before we reach the Ellerslie, we see steep gullies that streak down through the clearcuts where no new trees have regenerated naturally, let alone been replanted by the industry, as is the law.

Suddenly a channel narrows, swallowing our tiny boat between two rain-softened mountains. The mist hovers on a straight-edged elevation line two hundred feet above sea level, making it look as if the top of the world has been sawed off. The sea glows silvery gray

---

[3] Scott A. Elias, *The Ice Age History of Alaska's National Parks,* (Washington, D.C.: The Smithsonian, 1955).

with salmon backs as thick as rain. I know that just twenty miles inland, blue hanging glaciers hover one thousand feet in the air. Out from under their airborne lips launch frothing white projectiles of glacial water. They end up down here, sending the swirling, milky turquoise of ground-up peaks into the dark channels.

Such is this wild interface, termed the hypermaritime, where sea becomes land and land becomes sea.

An Untouched Yosemite

It has been raining softly all day. Halfway up the western coast of British Columbia, we enter the mysterious Ellerslie Watershed. The Ellerslie waterfall and rapids serve as dragon and gateway to this expansive half-domed fjordland. From rumors of previous travelers, we believe that its interior holds both archaeological and biological treasures. At the fjord's entrance, however, glaring, high-graded, vertical clearcuts made by small logging operators, called gyppos by industry and government alike, slash the continuous forest causing massive landslumps that expose the bedrock.

Baden tucks the forty-one-foot sailboat into the Ellerslie Channel near the rapids guarding an inner lagoon. The Ellerslie Watershed's rapids and waterfall, a geographic blockade to the inner passage, appear to me as an insurmountable challenge before we may enter the watershed's magnificent interior.

It is late in the day when three of us zoom off in the Zodiac for a quick look at the waterfall at the top of the lagoon. To cross Ellerslie Rapids, the narrow, shallow, rocky neck through which the guts of the sea are trying to pass to the other side of the Earth, we must disembark and line the heavy Zodiac through. Pulling the heavy boat wouldn't be so bad except the rock is slick with fucus and black algae. Our feet find no traction. Finally, we are through the rapids.

We are dismayed: The raw power of the ragged-toothed water plunging down three hundred feet of bedrock blocks any further penetration. What the waterfall does not have in grace, it makes up in sheer volume. Half the lifeblood of the interior is gushing out through this waterfall. My companions, Ian and Peter, who prefer to explore the wilderness at speed, push up the quiet lagoon straight to the steep rock face of the waterfall. Sane human beings would search for a worn trail, but the two men tie up under the waterfall and begin to climb.

I tilt back and gape straight up an immense gray wall that is constantly splashed by the waterfall: Climbing it will mean scrambling up a face of ominous stone covered with slippery algae, white water thundering nearby. The men scramble right up, and I follow more slowly.

The handholds and footholds are narrow and slippery with trickling water, yet I finally make it up. Solitude and grand beauty are my reward.

At the top of the waterfall, I enter a remnant of untouched rain forest. Lying between the mowed-down Olympic National Forest of Washington and the ice-locked fjords of Alaska, this land provides the fragile key to understanding the alchemy of transformation from solid ice to lush forests. From the Alaska Range down through the British Columbia Coast Range, the grandeur rises, later subsiding as it reaches toward Washington's coastline. Having been a national park ranger in Glacier Bay and Kenai Fjords national parks of Alaska, I long to understand how the transition between Alaska and the Lower Forty-Eight actually transpires—not from books, but by the seat of my pants, which I now apply to the polished slickrock at the lip of the falls. Thirteen inches from the water's tongue, this perch is thrilling.

Unknown, unrecorded, uncharted except by the native nations whose sacred land this is and now by an indomitable timber industry.

My companions have hurried off to explore. Without pressure from the men to travel quickly, I can absorb this marvelous power. At midlife, I still climb, kayak, backpack, chop wood—only slower than previously. Ian is in his early twenties with boundless muscle capacity, and Peter is in his fifties, in good shape and driven by a need to appear heroic before the public and the politicians. Peter's personality quirks, if they work to save the original forests, work for me. I resign myself to Peter's dislike of my nature: Tolerance is not reciprocal. My Emily Dickinsonian character now squats stock still in a scooped out rock basin where glaciers have burnished smooth the granitic rock. I try to write but am only able to gape and listen.

The bedrock gleams as fresh-oiled skin: buttocks, breasts, biceps of Earth. Right next to the water's thunder, my bones feel its vibration as it pounds down one stone shelf after another. Logs seven feet wide are tossed like tinder at the lip of the falls. Little is left once they go over. I imagine myself in a canoe, plunging over the edge, and run this image like a movie—over and over and over again.

Penetrating the Ellerslie

The next morning, we motor to the worn trail at the right of the waterfall. We must portage two small boats up three hundred feet and a quarter mile past the falls. Disassembling both boats, carrying all the parts and the two eight-hundred-pound engines up a quarter-mile steep trail is extremely hard work. All of us sweat while dreaming of thin ledges holding goat feet on tall granite faces. This is a harsh country to enter, but such exertion is a pittance to pay for such beauty.

I am the first to set off, carrying a tall green river bag full of equipment. With head down, grunting, I forget to be afraid. Alone, I run smack into a young black bear. Having not seen humans before, he cannot get his feet to work fast enough for escape. He falls all over himself. I laugh out loud, trying to respect his dignity but making a poor job of it.

The trail twists up tall steps and then down into a bog. Finally, we have hauled all the pieces up.

What a vision! A long lake winds off into the unknown. On all sides rise magnificent Yosemite-type Half Domes, faceted spurs of mountains sliced in half by ice over thousands of years. They loft from the water in sheer walls. It is Yosemite National Park, with all the traffic jams, concession stands, and maddening throngs drowned in eight hundred feet of water. Silent, wild, pristine.

I am stunned by the beauty of the sun beaming off the wet domes like headlights, of the granite swilled from the western flank of updoming bedrock at the continent's edge. The topography is far more dramatic than the North Cascades of Washington. Extensive mountain building heaved up cordilleras, which, in turn, caught the airborne Pacific Ocean on its way across North America and built ice domes so massive that they depressed the land. These huge cordilleras not only made their own weather but carved their own topography using the Ice Age as their chisel.

We glide up a singular arm of the hundreds of U-shaped valleys carved down the western edge of the coastal dome: From the Chilcotin territory on the east to these deep fjords on the west, only a few drainages cut clear through.

Although complex layers of sedimentary and metamorphic rock once lay on top of the cordillera, here the carving is so deep that it exposes the very core of the Earth that formed of the molten rock resolidifying. A fine, white granite.

Ground up into fine particles, this granite creates smooth crescent beaches of white sand that punctuate the sheer cliffs rising straight up from the water. We disembark on a sand shelf that drops off straight down into the deep fjord. The men, entirely focused on finding signs of grizzly bear, take off with the video camera. From here, I can see 250-foot-tall snags, or giant dead trees, sticking high into the skyline, gnarled and fluted with holes for woodpeckers or sylvan pipers.

I stand at the edge of a giant forest, almost afraid to enter. The forest, which ends suddenly only a few yards from the fjord, appears to me as a solid wall of twisting, rotating, gyrating, and ghoulish vegetation. I meander up the dry creek channel, an opening tunnel into a forest choked with eight-hundred-year-old trees. Everything is gigantic. Everything is covered with green. Six-foot ferns arch over my head. Huge, graceful fallen roots create archways and cavities through which I crawl like a tiny vole. Soon all is dark, yet, from above, green light floods through a stained-glass cathedral. Even my skin glows softly green. In essence of ancient forest: so dark and so light simultaneously.

Above me, interlocking devil's club leaves twenty inches wide spread horizontally into the backlit, vegetative dome. I see a veined Michelangelo ceiling.

As if cathedral stained glass lofting above me were not enough, the intricacy of the underworld captures me. Mosses, liverworts, and lichen creep, curl, and crenulate a world just as potent as that of the grizzly bears. Nine-foot-diameter western red cedar stumps tower above me, the trees cut by early loggers at heights of five to seven feet. Using misery whips, or two-man saws, they stood on springboards driven into the trunks five to seven feet above the ground so they could cut the trunks at a more manageable width. I scramble up immense roots that arch high over the memory of disintegrated nurse logs. These flying buttress roots fill the understory with gestures of giant gnomes. In my peripheral vision, all of the stumps are animated with mouths, knothole eyes, broken twig noses.

Everywhere I am caught off guard by troll mouths and root fists. Epiphytes drape in dark loops. Sphagnum moss swallows my legs up the calf. Velvet opera curtains hang above me. Berry vines drape, coil, and tear at my clothing—black-, blue-, salmon-, goose-, and huckleberry. Leathery liverworts splay out in circles of worn hide.

An exuberant, two-foot-thick carpet of sphagnum moss covers the forest floor and all of the downed logs with red and green star bursts the size of fingernails. *Sphagnum imbricatum* and *warnstorfii* create a tapestry of pale chartreuse, gold rusts, and burgundy. *Peltigera* liverworts wave fleshy, overlapped fingers. *Philontis fontana* club mosses mimic the tall conifers in half-inch, glaucous tufts. *Racomitrium lanuginosum* flows like pale-green ruffled feathers down each log.

How different this lush world is from the dry, gray and black cryptogams of the Arctic. The cryptogams here tell a different story than the tall conifers that tower above them do. They tell a story of nitrogen-poor, acidic soils, which underlie most all of the shadowy boreal forests in temperate, cool-wet climates. Sphagnum tells of semiterrestrial, water-logged bogs in loose talus piles. From the colorful sphagnum moss, I can surmise that the giant, ancient trees have their roots hooked around talus brought down by the glacier.

The timber industry would have us believe these are rich soils out of which giant trees spring within decades. These are thin, acidic soils—if there is any soil at all.

I stand here, where the Heiltsuk people were "created" so long ago. Their lives, over thousands of years, were so entwined with the mounds of moss and fungi, with giant fish, and with the immense spruce that it is easy for me to understand how a complex human culture arose.

The Heiltsuk lexicon consists of bracken, great trees, multitudinous fish, and giant brown bears. The ecosystem is their mythology, and the stories, their syntax. Yet life has not been easy for either human or plant: Ecosystems do not easily invent themselves in slim, acid soils. What has taken a millennia to evolve might soon be slashed to the ground.

The men return unsuccessful from their brown bear search. Unfortunately, no bear has eaten the video camera. The men have blithely reached the conclusion that the ecosystem has not yet developed to a sufficient abundance and complexity to support the great brown bears. This is still the realm of black bear, the men tell me conclusively.

I doubt it.

We float deeper and deeper inland in the Zodiac, not knowing what we will find. All around us, vertical avalanche chutes stripe the deep green mountains with bright green deciduous trees. The occasional giant spruce or western red cedar rising high above the forest canopy suggests a forest relatively untouched by human saw. These massive individuals, which stand high up in drainages, had been too hard to take out by hand with nineteenth-century tools. Early in the twentieth century, men with a crude form of A-framing high graded the best trees down by the shore, leaving us only glimpses of how huge these trees once grew.

Exorbitantly high, long slabs of fresh, unoxidized rock are continually exposed on the fjord walls as enormous conchoidal flakes exfoliate over time. These must set off waves shooting down and up the narrow fjord and rising thirty feet on the cliff walls. I imagine myself fishing quietly on the flat mirror surface, the calm broken only by the gentle rings of a fish kissing the surface. I imagine looking up and suddenly seeing building-size mounds of water heading my way. I imagine how I would drop my line and grab my paddle just in time to swing the canoe bow around into the wave. I imagine the bow plowing into the wave like a needle. I imagine it popping out and me sailing up over the wave and down the other side, only to do it again—and again—and again.

"Do you want any cookies?" Ian waves the package at me.

What? At this time?

I'm air-canoeing, he realizes and smiles. I grab a cookie and gaze upward again.

Such thoughts take my breath away.

High in a granite grotto, I spy a sudden flush of life on a sheer stone face: Berries spring out of bare rock; mosses grow in an exquisite palette of chartreuse, gold, and pearl against the dull gray face. Roots shoot far down into granite cracks, exfoliating the rock by pushing out until a fifty-foot flake crashes down. The logic of a quarter-inch root.

Huge, juicy cumulus clouds swirl over our heads in time-lapse motion. The sun is a cool disk sliced by a raven. I feel the afternoon wind intensify as it blows up the seven-mile-long trough lake, beating against us. We pass old timber cuts all along the fjord. Cables that once brought down ten-foot-wide spruce now rust on gray stone like varicose veins.

In winter, mountain goats descend all the way down to these waters to find nourishment.

Far above us, the raven carves gyres in the air, croaking archaically. Below us, abundant cutthroat trout that miraculously made it up the waterfall, probably flopping from ledge to ledge, are spreading their genes upland. I would love to splice some of their rambunctious genes onto my own, but if I missed by even one DNA letter, I might end up with a craving for flies.

Humans are not lacking a similar rambunctious compulsion to spread. Twenty years ago, a German family climbed the falls to homestead and clearcut a north arm of the Ellerslie Fjord. The Heiltsuk natives found them here the next winter, starving, and saved their lives. When spring came, they hurried back to Europe, never to return.

Suddenly, from the Zodiac, we spy a startling white hut against the backdrop of green wilderness on the north edge of Ellerslie Lake. We putter up to it cautiously, not wishing to disturb any people who might be about, and yet curious. New pots, pans, and gas cans tell us that the place is occupied.

Out of the hut walks a very surprised Norwegian, although his face shows no emotion. He is a tall, weather-beaten Nordic man in his early sixties with the movement of a native. We glimpse a younger Heiltsuk woman behind him inside the hut. He greets us softly, saying that his name is Larry Jorgenson and that he's been here fifteen years, having adopted his wife's way of life. He tells us he teaches at the community college in Bella Bella and has tried to warn his adopted people about what will happen to their forests. He says that because the forests have been here since the beginning of time, no Heiltsuk believes that they could ever be gone. He feels like a fish describing the desert to his Pacific cohorts.

Our leader, Peter, the Anglo with political strings, has been to the regional forestry office as recently as last spring and has seen photostatic copies of plans to begin roading the winter of 1992 and clearcutting in 1993.

Looking into Larry's unmoving face while Peter reveals the Forest Service's plans is like watching a young person die uselessly. Only it will not be one person. It will be an entire culture.

Larry tells us that his sister-in-law, Polly Waterfall, a healer and well-educated woman, does not believe something like this will happen. She does not believe that the government will cut down a First Nation's forest.

He tells us that Johnny Waterfall, her husband and the owner-operator of Wag Airlines, does not believe this either. They are pillars of the Heiltsuk community and have much influence. We suddenly feel cold and wet in the Zodiac.

The Heiltsuk tell us that they do not know that the rest of their sacred territory—the pristine Beautiful Lake, Walker Lake, Four Lakes, Sunny Island, and Mount Kees—is scheduled for slaughter.

Fisher Channel. Hole in the Wall. All will be gone.

The Heiltsuk cannot imagine that their government will do something so terrible. It is impossible, they say. After all, how could you destroy the center of the cosmos.

"I keep on telling my son you'd better get up here now because it won't be here long," says Larry Jorgenson.

The Band Council is thinking more positively. They believe the Forest Service won't cut the forests if the area has other economic viability. They plan to introduce sockeye fry to the fjord jointly with the B.C. Fisheries, another part of that same government. They are carefully counting escapement, measuring how many fish make it in and out of the Ellerslie. They have just begun the slow, painstaking process of studying what happens when a fish species is introduced into a system whose natural evolution from the Ice Age is just coming ready to accept fish fry. They want only to enhance a natural process. It will only be a few more years.

Studies take time.

But time is not what the Heiltsuk have. The band leaders do not know this. Those who have repeatedly asked the B.C. Forest Service what is planned for this magnificent sacred valley have repeatedly been told that there are no plans to cut. They have been blatantly lied to. Those of our crew who have been to the regional Forest Service office and demanded to see the maps know this.[4]

The Ellerslie: Ancestral Ground

Larry Jorgenson, a scholar of the Heiltsuk mythology, begins telling us stories. He tells the story of the Great Creation Flood of the Heilt-

---

[4] Since our trip in 1992, clearcutting plans have been put on hold because environmentalists, Natives, and politicians raised such a ruckus. In 1992 the Ellerslie Heiltsuk were in immediate danger of losing their ancestral forest.

suk, which took place in this very fjord. If the circumstances were not so grim, I would be having a good time. Storytelling between different peoples is one of the greatest human inventions and binds us together. Storytelling, like language, grows right out of these trees.

Larry tells us that one finds, throughout this fjord system, over one hundred documented archaeological sites: rock art, dwellings, paintings, burials, hunting camps.

The Ellerslie's sixty-four thousand hectares hold the origin stories of not just one, but four separate native groups and the interface of the Coastal and Inner Fjordland cultures. This valley is the spiritual center of four distinct cultures.

Peter, who would rather lecture than listen, grows impatient with Larry's story. He begins, "Based on the modus operandi of well-documented examples on Vancouver Island, people from the timber industry will come into your village and gather up three or four elders for a town meeting. During this meeting, they will announce the destruction of the forest that sustains your band. They will spread out their maps in a church basement during the day when the decision-making, English-speaking tribal members are off working. The timber industry will say, 'This is how we will clearcut the forest. We can do this because it is our legal right, because the British Columbian government gave us the tree farm license. If you get in our way, we can sue you for millions of dollars based on the profit we will forfeit. Is there any small adjustment you would like us to make?'"

Peter pauses for only a moment and then: "The timber company will have done its homework well. Before the meeting the company will call up the elders to find out where the grandest stands of trees are. They will know the best trees to cut."

Peter is not through lecturing. "The Haisla on Vancouver Island blocked the entrance of B.C. Tel in a huge tract of Ancient Forest," he says. "They said they would die rather than let the logging trucks in. The logging trucks were allowed in anyway, and their way of life is almost gone."

"The problem," explains Larry Jorgenson, "is focusing people's energy. They don't think it could happen to the land of their ancestors because the ancestors won't allow it."

Larry Jorgenson turns northeast and points.

"The meadow at the end of the lake turns into a marsh and then into a trail that goes in half domes all the way back up like diamonds to the hanging glaciers. My sister-in-law Polly Waterfall gathers medicinal plants and teaches people to heal with them."

And then Larry tells us my favorite story, a story of a great heroine, a Heiltsuk woman who saved all her people from ravaging outsiders. I would have to carry the story with me down to the waterfall to relive it because Peter is anxious to go.

It is time to leave Larry and his people to digest our terrible news. As we motor off, we turn around to watch Larry and his wife's father floating gently out in a dory. They look like a Courbet painting. They are pulling out kokanee and cutthroat as fast as one dips water from a bucket.

Going Home Saddened

On our way home to the *Sinbad* we pull up under rock faces that lean out over us. We cannot figure out how the ancestors painted so high up on the cliffs. The trees grow right down to the water's edge indicating that there was no isostatic rebound here.[5]

Yet, fifteen feet above our Zodiac are blood-red concentric circles, fourteen dots around three figures, lines splayed like huge fingers, and curvilinear meanders ("snakes") in segments.

My companions conjecture meaning from these waving lines and dots, stiffened stick figures holding or wearing odd protrusions, but I discourage them. Snakes do not live here. My archaeological work helping to record the last of over three thousand rock art sites in Chaco Canyon, New Mexico, trained me to avoid such culture-bound explanations.

---

[5] In isostatic rebound the land rises up as it is released from the weight of the great ice sheet.

The slosh of the deep black fjord, the heavy smell of water and forest, and the subtle hues of ancient pigment enchant us—exquisite rust reds and golds on white granite faces with golden stains over ancient paintings. Much of the surface has fallen into the lake, unrecorded, never to be seen again. Some pictographs are covered by a mosaic of moss or algae stain. We float the Zodiac along an immense white wall that plummets straight down into the deep water.

I am saddened that so little archaeological work has been done here. Ian says that according to the survey archaeologists have completed, the pictographs are at least two hundred years old. Although experiments with the pigment's chemistry that simulate weather conditions are not very accurate, they indicate that the yellow, black, and red ochres mixed with animal fat could last for over four hundred years.

The series of circular dots seems ceremonial to me, a counting, a marking, rather than the literal visual image. While the two men in the Zodiac reach for interpretations, I sit daydreaming of the ritual, the passageways into transcendent states of mind: Are these icons captured by a healer in a trance?

The Ancient Ones are tangibly present in spirit. They will last forever. It's the ancestors' bodies I do worry about, living restlessly by the hundreds in burial caves in overhanging cliff cavities. Because only the rock directly under the paintings is protected by law, clearcutting will destroy hundreds of grave and camp sites. Does the timber industry really think it can get away with grave desecration with impunity?

The Final Story

As we approach the roaring waterfall, my heart trembles. When and where will the current's invisible claw grasp our boat and sling us over? Larry's final story of the Heiltsuk ancestor comes to us now as a lifeline:

> The early Heiltsuk often fought with and lost to the warlike Haida
> from out on the coast. The Haida were a fierce people who attacked

often, taking many of the band for slaves and killing all others. The Haida warriors once captured a strong Heiltsuk woman and carried her away. She thought sadly of all her people who would be killed or who would die.

She directed her conquerors down the long fjord lake we now call the Ellerslie toward this very waterfall. She knew the lake intimately, and could hear the roar of the waterfall long before the Haida could. She directed them toward it, saying, "Here is the proper landing place for the trail around the waterfall." At the very moment the current first grasped the Haida warrior canoe, she tipped it over, dumping all the warriors into the devouring current. She remembered a snag log that jutted far out from the right side just above the fall. Swept toward it at incredible speed, she grasped it at the final moment and pulled herself along it until she could crawl out just above the falls.

From her precarious position on the log, she could hear the Haida warriors screaming as they were sucked over the upper lip of the waterfall and ground into bloody pulps. Her bravery saved all her people from death or slavery.

Once again, it seems that we need her desperately.

Namu

51°53' N, 127°53' W

*B*ack on the *Sinbad*, we gas up at Bella Bella and head twenty miles south to Namu. Namu means whale, but this is a village of herring. When we first glimpse Namu, it appears to be a pristine village of layers upon layers of bright white dormitories so well maintained that we expect to see the steep wooden stairs up the hillside teaming with young fish-processing workers in rubberized coveralls.

Yet, except for a handful of folk, it is abandoned. The herring were overfished decades ago. When we pull up, no one appears. There seems to be absolutely nothing moving up there—until I raise my binoculars and see two black eyes moving.

A ways up the mountainside, in one of the many abandoned buildings, two hooded eyes watch me. Later, the man shows up near the dock, secluding himself from our direct gaze as if we might melt him. He stares at us sadly. A one-time fisherman, he is a heavyset, bearded man in his forties. I wonder why he isolates himself here. He continues to scrutinize us women—Karen, Cindy, and I. He moves his eyes slowly up and down the two younger women, examining them like a starved man would food.

The cannery, now shut down, reminds us that herring are just a memory. We wander in silence past mammoth steaming drums for fish, past draconian pipes and valves the size of my torso, past rusted gears and cogs the size of tractor tires, past broken-down fish processors, past the macabre memories. Where telephones once were, wires stick out of empty walls.

Bright white dormitories with red or green trim march up the hills, hundreds of transient ghosts in their beds. Brought in to process millions of pounds of marine life year after year, their tenants seem to have just left. One clean, fluorescent-lit prefab is now the only town store. Its brightly colored boxes, dwarfed by the huge warehouse proportions of the building, huddle together on the mostly empty shelves: raucous-colored refugees from the excesses of the Lower Forty-Eight. Ostentatious overpackaging in a town about poverty and abandon.

The bearded, lonely man shows up near the ripped-out telephones. He will not speak to us three women; he only stares as if we are a strange species whose sounds he cannot make out. He continues to devour the two younger women with his eyes; they ignore him. Feeling his dismay in what age brings, I gaze at him openly and grin. He reads the words printed on my chest:

FORTY ISN'T OLD
IF YOU'RE A TREE.

He smiles shyly but quickly catches himself and turns away.

We climb up the long planks of stairs and then back on a long shoulder of mountain where a rickety boardwalk protects us from falling in the bog underneath. When we reach Namu Lake, the other two strip off their clothes and go swimming. I am more cautious. The lake water is almost black, and the lake snakes off into a mist-shrouded distance where monsters squeeze out from under glaciers, ravenous for unwary nature writers. Finally, I submerge my body, which turns bright yellow in the water. All of my pores are washed clean, and I am glad for this refreshing bath—the tiny shower on the boat allows us only short squirts of water.

When we depart, I turn to search for the bearded man. He is in his cottage with the binoculars again, watching us walk out of his life forever. We gaze back at the village of Namu.

Although from a distance Namu looked pristine, on closer inspection we saw it was not. The rusting storage tanks two stories high, the mounds of junk piled in abandoned yards, remind me of all places lived in by transient workers who do not dare to care about a place—

a place they will leave when the resource is mined. As in logging camps, transients pass seasonally.

This was not home. It never could be home, just something awful to bear. No cans of cheerful geraniums graced the steps of the dwelling, as in Mexico, to break the monotone of poverty. Some of the buildings are makeshift board structures so ugly that the numbest laborer must have felt gnarled within them. The loss of caring for beauty in the name of quick resource extraction rivals war in its ability to destroy nature and the human soul.

An anthropology professor I had in college argued with me that a caring for beauty comes only after the physical needs of a people are met. Yet comparative anthropological studies from all over the world indicate that people who must struggle to survive hold aesthetic pleasure as high as other natural attributes and tie them closely to the spiritual nature of man and to the closeness of human bonds with nature.

In New Mexico, I learned of the Hopi concept of ceremonial glitter, where many beautiful colors waving represents the beauty of a world inhabited by spirits. The Navajo called it "to walk in beauty," meaning to know the land as being vitally alive and that you are part of it. Despite its well-kept buildings, Namu village does not walk in beauty.

The *Sinbad* now turns toward great Koeye Watershed. As we gain distance from land in the river, we see that Namu is set in a grandeur of mountains, ice fields, ancient rain forest, and surging Inside Passage waters.

We are sliding down to the sea along a forest of giant trees when the mist swallows us. We continue through its white viscosity toward, according to rumors, the most diversified watershed of our entire journey. The Koeye will surpass even our wildest imaginings.

The Dance of the
Great Brown Bears

51°48' N, 127°50' W

The Koeye

The *Sinbad* drifts along the continent's edge, which, as always, is enigmatic, inscrutable. The darkest, most completely zippered forest resists our gaze. I cannot imagine how we are to find the secretive gateway into the tiny bay that is the Koeye River's mouth. Along such a bleak coast, I am feeling alienated from the Canadians. In many subtle ways, they are communicating, "This is not your forest. You do not belong here. This is no concern of yours." Peter has crimped our schedule again, and I feel that I am a prisoner of time. Like the shoreline and its solid barrier of trees, there will never be an opening.

The essence of exploration is changing perceptions. Come to think of it, the same is true of this entire journey, my entire life. Something is soon to change. I'm hoping it will be my bleak attitude.

Suddenly the impenetrable forest along Fitzhugh Sound gulps, and we quickly tuck around Koeye Point. Our clearcut reconnaissance team glides into a magnificent blue-black bay with its smooth crescent of improbable white sand. Fresh water murmurs the susurration of eighty thousand acres of white bedrock grinding down. Every few seconds, a huge silver salmon leaps a foot out of the water, thirty-five pounds of flying fish flesh.

Ian tells us that we have come here to examine the mystery of eighteen deeply entrenched footprints, known as the Brown Bear Dance. The long trek we will make up the Koeye's lakes, bogs, and shallow riverbeds will be worth it if we can unravel the secret of the bear's ritual.

The Koeye Watershed is a very special place, one of four significant, untouched watersheds of mid-coast British Columbia: 79,429 acres as yet unlogged in 1992. The other three untouched watersheds are the Khutzymateen, the Kynock, and the Kitlope. The Kitlope, the most northerly stands of merchantable timber, had been planned for clearcut in 1993 but has since been protected. The Khutzymateen, where clearcutting was once a hot and contentious issue, has since been saved. The Kynock is protected within Fiordland Provincial Park. The fate of the Koeye remains unsealed.

The Koeye, like all of the other deep coastal fjords, goes from sea level up to eight thousand feet, to the great hanging glaciers of the Coast Range. But the Koeye is the only fjord system to also include a large segment of Hecate Lowlands on the Inside Passage. Thus, this biogeographic system holds the key to our understanding a fully functioning ecosystem from alpine peak to sea.

That the Koeye has not been preserved as a world treasure will be incomprehensible to future generations. It includes white sand beaches unusual to this coast, twenty miles of gentle river, two huge lakes, numerous small tributaries, an extensive estuary, and a sandy-bottomed bay once full of crabs though now overharvested. Exceptional hypermaritime rain forest hovers over the Koeye's banks.

I am anxious to get my feet on Hecate Lowlands: glacier-scraped bedrock covered with bogs of sphagnum, shrubs, and stunted forest. On thin acidic soil clings an implausible but hardy krummholz of red cedar, hemlock, shore pine, juniper, and amabilis fir (Pacific silver fir to us Americans), all slinging their arms out in the same direction due to the high velocity winds.

Close by the *Sinbad*, twenty-seven endangered marbled murrelets float unafraid, an extended family of football-shaped seabirds mottled gray and pearl. In Puget Sound, I always feel incredibly fortunate to see even a sole individual of these once abundant birds. They prefer to nest in old growth conifers that are two hundred feet high, a habitat that is rapidly disappearing around Seattle. In the states, we have been able to use the Endangered Species Act to slow some of the clearcutting along the coast; here in Canada people have no such powerful, federal tool.

Across the bay, the motley crew of a rusty junk ship pull up empty crab pots. Ring-billed gulls, loons, kingfishers, and grebes chortle as unabashedly as if we have sailed into an intimate gathering of old friends. Far too few urban human ears are privy to such beautiful cacophony. Far too few humans have documented such incredible abundance.

At the request of the Sierra Club of Western Canada, Wayne and Erica McCrory carried out a season's worth of reconnaissance-level fieldwork in the lower estuary of the Koeye during one week of September 1990. They recorded abundant beaver, great blue heron, geese, harlequin, loon, osprey, Peale's peregrine falcon, merlin, ruffed grouse, surf birds, ruddy turnstone, wandering tattler, greater yellow-leg, pigeon guillemot, phalarope, rhinoceros auklet, Bonaparte's gulls, ravens, and crows. Through thick shrub they followed chick-adees and brown creepers, ouzels, winter wrens, and fox sparrows. They found mink, river otters, seals, sea lions, and all five species of Pacific salmon thriving in great quantities. Upriver, the McCrorys watched (and ate) Dolly Vardens and cutthroat trout.

Sitting in one spot, Wayne saw sea lions, harbor seals, and a hump-back whale breaching in the outer channel, as well as land and marine birds thick in the sea and air and wolves and a magnificent brown bear prowling on the white beach.

Erica wrote this of the mystery the Canadians and I were seeking: "Twenty miles up the fjord where the river becomes too shallow for a boat, a deeply grooved trail has been danced upon for thousands of years by great brown bears. The eighteen-print-long 'rhythm trail' indicates that bears fall into a repetitive pattern of walking exactly on old steps so each paw print deepens and deepens."

Karen, Ian, and I are mad with desire to see those prints. In particu-lar, Ian, our young photographer, is driven to document them on film.

"But there may be grizzlies still *in* the tracks," I comment.

"Yeah!" grunt the men in unison and great anticipation.

The lushness of the Koeye is a hint of the original biomass of North America that now exists only in slim fragments in the Lower Forty-Eight. At eighty thousand acres, the Koeye is large enough to be ecologically self-sustaining and, therefore, to contribute to the world's understanding of untampered forest. Undisturbed, the Koeye could provide a benchmark for biologists, ecologists, pedologists, hydrologists, and resource managers.

Soon I stand beneath a thick weaving of epiphytes draped on Western red cedar limbs. The red cedars split at their tops like multiple sailing masts, three or four prongs each, in the acidic bog soil. Botanists cannot explain why. The hemlocks I pass, with their drooping tops, are uniform in age, the stand having been cut about forty years ago. Something feels wrong to me here: Perhaps it is the even-aged stands which have notably less diversity and, therefore, less life.

In nature, trees reestablish themselves in uneven succession as an individual tree falls over. In a natural forest, as one old giant crashes down in a storm, leaving a hole in the canopy, in rush nitrogen-fixing shrubs, a miniature ecosystem of new plants and animals. In the hole, a maelstrom of microclimate swirls between the ground and the canopy carrying the seed and spore of new life: epiphyte, fungi, and vascular plant. In a clearcut, regeneration creeps in only slowly from the sidelines. The world-record clearcuts on Vancouver Island, visible from the space shuttle, spell disaster for the regeneration of all species.

Back on the beach I find so many tracks I can hardly put a foot down without treading on one. When Peter putters up to retrieve me in the Zodiac, I can't wait to tell him of the proliferation of life.

I gush, "Gull, sandpiper, mink, river otter, goose, mallard, harlequin, vole, mouse, an eagle killing and eating a gull, one loon, and, that most magnificent of fellow travelers, Brother Bear!"

"There was only *one set* of prints, and that was quite old," he snaps coldly, impatient with my misinformation. I am at a loss. I still haven't learned that the only track worthy of mention is that of the brown bear. I have often observed this endangered species tunnel vision among my own species, *Homo Enviromentalipoliticolus*, but up here—amidst all this diversity—it is shocking. Videotape psychosis: the love of close-up shots of giant warm fuzzies, enthrallment with megafauna at the expense of the microorganism, a passion for the animal kingdom over the lowly plant kingdom. Motto: If it walks proudly, kills swiftly, and shits big, film it. If it lies there at the base of the food chain like slime—forget it! Peter, whose role model is David Attenborough, has difficulty imagining the host of the popular television series kneeling in front of a scrambled-egg slime mold extolling its virtues.

I have always loved areas on maps that remain unknown to me. The coastal mountains of British Columbia are such an unknown.

Life is most abundant here at the greatest extremes, because of the rapid fluctuations in water volume and salinity due to heavy precipitation, in the sudden melting of distant ice fields by warm rain, in the breaking of ice dams seven thousand feet above. The waves surging inshore from a storm on the Pacific Ocean bring up the saline count. Periodically tsunamis flatten the coastlines. How does life survive such extremes? I am reminded of Stephen Jay Gould's theory of punctuated equilibrium in evolution. In punctuated equilibrium, the evolution of new species is not on a continuous, even curve but is in a series of wipeouts and resurgences, like stair steps.

Here, this geography is not only punctuated, it has been punched, wiped, ground, and drenched with great persistence.

From ice field and solidly frozen tundra down to the biological soup of the Pacific, the brown bear needs it all.

We putter up the rich biological soup of the river past twenty-seven bald eagles perched in the tops of old conifers. Turnstones and surf birds flush so thickly that they block sight of shore. Air, earth, and river are solid with spiraling nutritional loops, with trophic energy chains. The wild Koeye is thumping, humping, and pumping with life.

This ancient, pristine river, a river like no other I have ever seen, pulls us into the heart of the continent. We are plunging back two centuries into a time when Earth was in the full flush of biodiversity. I am falling down a time tunnel past a myriad of life-forms, a biobath of genetic stirrings. Forty or fifty female mergansers ball themselves up and fly squawking up the river. Thousands of small fish team under the Zodiac. The water depths wrinkle and glitter like aluminum foil.

Like all other unlogged watersheds in mid-coast British Columbia, the Koeye lacks an adequate biological inventory or meaningful ecological assessment. Karen and I, aware of our responsibility if this watershed is soon to be clearcut, want to do what we can to inventory it, but Peter wants to move swiftly. I would be perfectly thrilled with a stack of guidebooks, food, my tent, and three months alone up any one of these rivers. Speed! Urban man's neurosis.

A dead crab a mile upriver marks the fluid edge between clear and saline water. The river flattens, intensifying its mosaic-patterned cobble. Magnified, these bottom boulders are complex, unusual Coast Range granites. We float silently, having to rely on paddles because of the shallow bottom. Peter is impatient when we abandon the motors, but Karen, Ian, and I find the silence awe inducing. The sploosh-drip, sploosh-drip of paddles. No words.

The stream bends east into a rust-colored salt marsh.

Ahead, a small tributary enters from the dark forest. The water has mysterious riffles. The inky surface is knifed with thousands of serrated blades slicing in all directions. As the water deepens where the side channels have carved out the river bottom, the riparian character transmutes to deep water life. The saline plants disappear, and terrestrial detritus flows down from the forest in a forest smoothie.

We slide silent as owl wings over the machining surface, the churning caused by a thousand ten-inch salmon fry feeding and leaping, drinking in bugs and osterized forest like fraternity members drinking beer.

The trees are soda straws, drawing the sun's light and food into the gleaming river water. The fish drink them, too.

Soon, these salmon will leave their deep pools and fluid cafeteria to venture far out into the unknown sea. Twelve thousand black opal eyes will survey the channel as it widens in front of them. With their noses, they will sense the thrill of the incoming tide, pass the tilted separation of limestone layers underwater, and memorize the numerous limestone holes as if they were Hindu temple carvings. The fish will slide through submerged tree roots spun about like the arms and legs of Shiva dancing. Olfactory memories will be forming—an ichthyological mythology will rise in slippery brains.

Vivid rust-red sedges and reeds punctuated by lavender aster and white yarrow grow upriver. We beach in the cobbly shallows and stroll up the shore through sedges that reach up to our ribs. A grizzly bear has recently been digging holes every few feet in the meadow. Karen and I poke our hands in the holes, which are still damp. We glance up nervously every few seconds like deer. It is a strange sensation to be prey instead of predator.

Karen and I, both avid plant identifiers, stoop to examine what the bears have eaten. This, we think, might be important information not yet adequately recorded for the Koeye. We discover that in spring the bears devour deschampia, hairgrass, sedge, and fritillaria, and, of course, salmon. Awful-smelling salmon debris lies all along the river. And, emerging from their caves in spring, the bears also love to devour horsetails; full of silicate grist, they rasp out the winter's excrement and clean the alimentary chute.

I have watched a grizzly, or brown bear, glissade down snowfields, then scramble back up to glissade down again, savoring the sensation of ice and speed. These bears love to plunge into roaring streams where prayer-shaped, ready-to-eat pink flesh swims. Wriggling, claw-speared meat—no line necessary—just a swift arc of paw.

From subalpine clear down to sea level, a nine-thousand-foot relief, various ecosystems feed the bears. Each level is critical to their varied diet. The grizzly is a bear for all seasons. He dens in the high forest or snow in winter, then descends, licking his chops in the spring.

Five hundred to fifteen hundred pounds, cinnamon with darker ripples, Brother Bear is becoming a rare sight. His genetic diversity has been diminished; the animals will not cross clearcuts from river valley to river valley to mate. The scattered individuals are in danger of inbreeding.

Peter's obsession with brown bears is not unmerited: They are an indicator species because they need the ecological diversity of an entire river drainage from alpine to sea to survive. Even with an excellent federal recovery program, we have accepted the demise of a viable brown bear population in the Lower Forty-Eight. It is hard for me to discover that Canada, too, is no longer a bottomless pocket of wildlife, a pocket we Americans can pick at any time we destroy our own.

Brown bears are mighty travelers, crossing up to fifty miles of terrain a night on tundra, as well as strong swimmers. They easily swim the Inside Passage to Hunter and Calvert Islands twelve miles off the mainland. From a bear's sensibilities, this wetland is a veritable animal, vegetable, and mineral smorgasbord.

One treat for this big wooly stomach-on-legs is an umbel-shaped plant with carrot-like leaves, *Oenanthe sarmentosa*, or water parsley. Its root, sweet and crunchy, tastes like coconut with an incredible aftertaste that delights us humans. A fine ursine desert for our omnivorous friend. Its presence indicates wet, nitrogen-rich soils in cool climates. As my legs sink into the cold meadow muck, I gain a better grasp of the importance of wetlands: Their soils are far from the acidic bogs under the stunted boreal forests that so challenge all life. Instead, these wetlands are laboriously laying down a fertile legacy. It takes hundreds of years for the wetlands to build soil a few feet deep. In contrast, it may take only a month for a soccer-field-sized wetland to fill with silt from a clearcut.

Tonight is the night of a very bright moon. Holding up my hand, I can see its veins at midnight. I am worried. Our young photographer, Ian, will sling himself above the meadow in a tall cottonwood to sleep in a hammock. As we know from paw prints, a young bear will cavort right under Ian's tree.

"Brown bears do not climb trees," says Ian.

"But we will be asleep in *Sinbad* three miles away, unable to help," worries Karen.

"At least you will be able to videotape yourself being eaten," I say cheerfully. Ian pays me no mind.

I admire Ian's courage and perseverance a great deal and even find myself envious of his unusual acts of bravery. He plans to awaken predawn and photograph the young male bear fishing the river.

The next morning we anxiously motor back upriver from the *Sinbad*, wondering what we will find—only a shredded shirt and a broken camera? Instead, Ian has captured the young grizzly on film sweeping his paw through the water and, on first swipe, impaling a wriggling salmon.

"Probably a young bear moving into new territory," explains Ian.

As a group, we wander upslope through asters, sweetgrass, and yarrow—the primary successional stages of a swamp changing into a red alder thicket. Ridges run through the soggy meadow, rippling its back. On the ridges small groves of red cedar and a gnarly orchard of Koeye crabapple. Coastal natives made handles, bows, wedges, digging sticks, and halibut hooks from this highly resistant fruit wood. The halibut hooks had to be powerfully strong, able to hold a fish weighing up to two hundred pounds, and yet they were the loveliest of hand-held power objects.

Scat full of fresh blueberry and red huckleberry fiber increases. We fan out across the meadow cautiously, calling to each other loudly like Canada geese in flight. None of us carries a weapon; we each rely on our senses and staying keen.

Peter stops everybody and announces melodramatically, "Each of you chose to come here of your own free will. If you get eaten, you can't sue me." In grizzly territory the best policy is to remain alert and create lots of noise; many people travel in grizzly country.

"If I get eaten," I remind him, "I won't sue you, but I will ruin your trip."

We slowly enter a bower under a grove of red cedar. Frightened, I reason with myself that any self-respecting bear will be long gone—he knows of humans and guns. In British Columbia poaching is as prevalent as legal takes: The ratio is about one to one according to 1990 B.C. Fish and Wildlife estimates. Great White Cowards lay out rotting meat and then just pick the bears off. Hunting it is not: Humans don't eat grizzly meat.

Although we see no brown bears in the bower, we notice abundant and fresh signs of their passage.

Going to the Bear Dance

We paddle the two Zodiacs upriver as far as we can. When the water gets too shallow we get out one by one, slipping and laughing, and drag the boats along the large river cobble. My jeans are rolled up, but soon I am wet to the waist. There! Off on the bank, deep in the trees, eyes are watching us. Predators, particularly bears, will circle around humans unseen to track their own hunters.

When dragging the boats is no longer practical, we tie them to alder branches hanging over the river and climb up the muddy bank. The trail here is old and wide and smooth, but I follow closely behind Ian, who is carrying the bear spray. Looking at the map, we find that we have another eight miles to go. Our photographer wants to go on, to feel the presence of the immense bears. Karen, Cindy, Baden, and I also want to continue, realizing that this is a once-in-a-lifetime experience. So when our leader dictates that we must turn around so that he can continue hurrying down the coast to the politics in Victoria, we are disgusted. With this latest announcement, our research trip has been cut short by a month. I have given up a job to be here. Hot, angry words pass between father and son. I sit to the side, trying to appear invisible, trying to go well and graciously with whatever is decided. But I'm pissed as hell.

It is painfully frustrating to feel that we may be the last naturalists to penetrate these remote areas before they are clearcut. Three of us shed tears.

We never see the bear dance. We never know the answers we long for to so many questions:

What goes off in a brown bear's brain when he steps in those same steps of his ancestors? Is it coincidence? Yet they were too deep for coincidence. Is it intentional, since it requires concentration and physical exertion for the different-sized bears? Is it the very first urge toward dance? Was dance perfected in older mammalian minds long before humans evolved? Is rhythmic, exactly repeated movement emotionally satisfying to animals in some deep way?

Are these steps the forerunner to the dances that we all perform when we are ecstatic or aroused: dancing from leg to leg until a crazed, glazed look comes to the eye, moving the head up and down and croaking out a croon? Did such behavior spring into being long before we separated into bears and human beings?

On the way back down, we pause in the meadow to get a close look at a bear's day bed. Our leader informs us that the bears bed down during the heat of the day in a small grove of trees, just like those cedars up on the ridge. We approach cautiously, afraid, shouting to one another.

We enter one red cedar den through an arching canopy of boughs. Dappled with moving sunlight, surrounded by false lilies of the valley, wintergreens, and salal, padded with mosses and *Alectoria*, dripping tree lichens, this is a beautiful bower.

Against the oldest conifer a bear has slept and rubbed it smooth and raw: years and years of rubbing. Centuries of rubbing. Although abandoned, the day bed hushes us. Here was something that relatively few humans ever see: a brown bear day bed. We stand in awe.

Although this animal at the top of the food chain has been tortured by poachers after gall bladder, professional guides with mechanical advantage, bear baiters, and curious videotapers, he has never been tormented by the buzzing helicopter, the dart gun, the knockout drug hangover, the scale, the blood sucker, the radio collar, and the tooth yankers. If he had been, we would know more than what this abandoned day bed can tell us. We might know how many bears there are, how healthy they stay, and what habitat they require. Ignorance is bliss for the extraction industries.

But the day bed does tell us a lot. It tells us of an animal who lives in beauty, who walks in beauty, who eats deliciously, whose life is filled with sensuous pleasures, with wild rivers and meadows swollen with salmon fats, tangy fruits, juicy grubs, and vegetables, whose sky is forever varying, and whose vista from the top of the glacier-covered mountain this spring must have been absolutely magnificent.

Rivers Inlet South
to Cape Caution

51°35' N, 127°33' W
51°12' N, 127°47' W

*A*s we sail up Rivers Channel, the western red cedar close in on us and huge salmon leap all around. Night falls on Rivers Inlet, and we have an eery sensation of complete wildness.

Ian and Peter return from a short Zodiac excursion with a fifteen-pound salmon. Both Karen and Ian are vegetarians who feel that we eat too high on the ecological food chain. The men leave the huge fish for Karen to clean in the twelve-inch galley sink. The fish is slippery, the knives dull. Squeamish and bewildered, she turns and admits to me that she has never cleaned a fish before. I'm at my proper task of writing and not paying much attention. The pile of thirty mosses and liverworts in front of me is crying out to be identified. With hand lens, ink pot, pen, and nibs, and books spread out, I am in the middle of a taxonomic orgy.

After five minutes of drawing a pen and ink rendition of the lobes of a liverwort as seen through a hand lens, I hear a shriek and a thud. As Karen slipped the knife into the salmon near its neck, the salmon had squirmed and leapt into her arms.

"It's alive!" she screams, as if the fishermen and the universe have tricked her into cruelty.

She cries in pain for the salmon and lets me push her aside to kill the fish with a quick throat slit. The salmon now thrashes about on the galley floor, and I grapple her up to the counter. The fish continues to struggle, so I clutch her scales, then hug her full-bodied to my chest. There are fish guts up and down my fresh clothes, then on my face, and in my hair.

Karen cries out again as I slit open the belly and pull out a long scarf of red roe.

Thousands of three-eighth-inch eggs gleam in a pink plastic bowl—beings that are alive and should be swimming out to sea. Salmon are disappearing all up and down the western seacoast. They are already gone in parts of Europe and the East.

Karen begins to weep and weep. Then, much to my chagrin, I begin to weep. Never before in my years of catching Rocky Mountain rainbow trout have I felt anything less than elation in cleaning a fish. Karen has reframed my vision. I, too, now perceive this fish not as food but as a wild fishwoman, Sister Salmon. As Life-Bringing, River Saint, and Madonna Salmon. We need a proper Coast Salish First Salmon ceremony to honor her.

Captain Baden comes down the ladder, laughing gently at us. I feel like Lady Macbeth, with blood up to my armpits, blood all over the kitchen, blood sloshing in the sink. Guts are ground into my new silk-screen salmon sweatshirt. Out, out damned gut, I chant under my breath. Karen just sobs.

A trio of bloody females are we: a naturalist who shouldn't have cried, a spiritual non-flesh-eater who continues to cry, and a fish with an all-powerful need to deposit her roe.

I am thinking that the twenty-three-year-old is right. In Washington State much of the salmon industry has been shut down to allow salmon numbers to come back up and to save the many species that are near extinction. Siltification by clearcutting, damming, overfishing, and fish nuking at the Hanford nuclear site have just about finished off Washington's abundant wild salmon runs. In Newfoundland, fishermen by the thousands have met economic ruin and unemployment lines due to lack of fish.

I begin to think that our cook's reaction signals a higher step in the evolution of human consciousness. I am so confused, having had fine experiences of fly fishing in Colorado, yet also being a spiritual grandchild of Rachel Carson's silent springs and rivers. Karen is a very strong young woman, confident in her actions. Her reaction is no city-folk squeamishness. It represents a solid, profound, and spirited grasp of the future.

♫

Then, oh Lord, we hear Peter's raucous laughter above deck. Do we really need this? I look at Karen, who is bracing herself. Down the ladder he comes. Seeing this bloody mess of females bawling, he lets out a huge guffaw and says, "Oh, for God's sake, women, there's plenty of fish in the sea!"

Deep Channel, Deep Discussion

The next morning, I discover peace for the moment. The sway of water, the smell of wet air full of salmon entrails and mold, the early morning fog, the dark encroaching forest … all is very mysterious and otherworldly here at Dawson Landing. After yesterday's fish cleaning, Captain Baden and I left the fishermen to their frantic task of plucking the larger salmon out of the ancient fjords and brought the sailboat across Rivers Inlet and through the narrow crevice between Walbran and Edna islands to this little, everything-you-need-in-one-shack sort of landing.

Baden and I had tied up rather smoothly, I thought, considering my lack of sailing experience. Then we hurried to the store/gas station/garbage dump/rest stop. We bought out the store and sold the owners our garbage for a dollar a bag. The young owners were born up in these misty inlets. Isolation didn't matter to them.

"How's're fuel a-gulpin'?" the young husband asked Baden, who was wincing as he checked out the pump prices.

"Oh, fine. Just fine and dandy," said Baden.

"That's funny, I haven't tasted it myself," the owner responded. A strange sense of humor, I think, but our encounters with human strangeness were just beginning.

On the way back to our ship, we ran into Mr. and Mrs. Conspicuous Consumption on their yacht. Gregarious Americans, they already had a good start on their martinis.

"Hey there, little gal," Mr. American shouted in my general direction, all very friendly, "Put down all your junk there and come over here. I got a present for you."

Doing as I'd been bid, I leave oranges, pop cans, and cleaning products rolling about the *Sinbad's* galley counters and pop up on deck again. There, a giant salmon mouth, open and level with my nose, is grinning at me for all it is worth. It has been thrust in my face. Right away I grasp that this is an even bigger salmon than Ian's fifteen-pound prize.

"Take 'er. We caught too many. Can't ship 'em back from up in this godfersaken country. You young folk look good and hungry."

"Then why do you keep fishing them?" I blurt out angrily. I want to use the word "murder."

The American looks at me aghast. I can see that, for him, the question ranks up there with "Why is there air?" or "Who's your mama?"

"Here, take it," he says, thrusting this salmon at me again. He calls it a gift. I tell him about the fifteen-pounder that Ian caught just yesterday, saying that we already have too much meat. He takes it as an offense.

"This one's way bigger than that. Damn sight prettier too: Look at her coloring and firmness. She's a beauty."

So that's how I came to be standing on deck cradling an eighteen-pound female salmon in my arms in yet another clean shirt.

Baden comes around the corner, and I start apologizing. Although he had chuckled at our predicament yesterday, he is a fine sailor, and a good seaman hates the taking of extra fish life.

Yet suddenly he gets a gleam in his eye. I catch his drift which puts a gleam in my eye as well. If the fishermen hadn't been so God Almighty full of themselves for catching rockfish and salmon yesterday, and if Peter had not laughed at me, we might not have conceived of this plan.

Soon we hear the Zodiac buzzing up to the sailboat, and we nonchalantly go about our tasks. I hear Baden above me on deck, asking how their fishing luck was and hear negative grunts in response.

"Not only could we not get very far up Sandell Inlet to see the state of the virgin forest, but we didn't catch a thing. That fifteen-pounder will have to do for a while."

"Oh ... not really," says Baden in a laid-back manner. "Susan and I caught a little something just by casually throwing a line overboard."

"What!?" Peter's voice is incredulous. Outraged. Baden's saying that I, the non-sea-legged, lichen-headed dingbat, had achieved *anything* was having the impact that Baden and I had hoped for.

"Oh ... it's down on the counter. Don't think she's cleaned it yet so you guys could see it," Baden says. Ian and Peter shove their heads down the hole to see it.

"An eighteen pounder, eh?" says Baden casually.

We allow the fishermen to stew for a while in their emasculated indignity while I clean the second fish. Ian is in a very disgruntled mood because he had intended to take off in the Zodiac up Darby Channel on a solo overnight but the gas pump is shut down. Even after we tell them of the joke, the tension on the small sailboat, which really has room for only three, is nasty.

So the next morning, feeling all too close to too many piscine and humanoid companions, I slip out solo. It is pre-dawn, and I have poured a strong cup of coffee. All is right with the world. The old gray dock boards are creaking loudly as they move together and apart. Fish guts float nearby; a dark forest looms overhead.

Down from the forest slide five otters, all shiny and black, sleek as eelgrass. The otter family plays close to me, humorous, agile. Their great strength and suppleness delight me. A great blue heron, only his eye moving, stands stately nearby, one leg up.

I write in my journal until it is almost time to leave, then reluctantly return to the sailboat.

∾

By mid-morning, Captain Baden is motoring us through a narrow passage only a quarter-mile wide in spots, through broken islands and sunken rock. Although it is not an easy passage to navigate, it is here that the captain and I decide to have a gentle battle.

Baden begins secretively to confide in me, as if of some crime. Seems he has been fuming internally with the rage of a fine wooden-boat builder. He is angry about the stance of the five environmentalists on board: to never cut any more old growth under any circumstance. He had carefully crafted his beautiful sailboat from ancient red cedar and yellow cedar, using Douglas fir for the floors and beams. He had hand-picked each timber from Dogwood Lumber on Vancouver Island. The wood was sold to him by a Finnish dealer who has boats in his genes.

Baden has come to middle age with carpenter tools in his hands and a boat in his heart. With his own hands, he formed the sheer, or the shape of the ship, with western red cedar, which does not resist shaping. At only thirty-four pounds per cubic foot, it is excellent for thicker, lighter hulls. Red cedar has lots of air in it; that is why it's like a sponge on the forest floor and retains so much water for the forest. "You work with it green," confides Baden.

"Yellow cedar is denser," he says, "It's the famous boat-building material and now is almost extinct in southern B.C. I used teak, the classic boat-builder's wood, for the cosmetic touches. And I also used Honduras mahogany, which is now endangered in the Amazon. It's a nonresistant hardwood that finishes just beautifully for detailing."

He continues, telling me, "Jeulatong, from Southest Asia, covers the walls and surfaces. It's the blond wood that's laminated over the bulkhead, which is solid plywood. The bulkhead walls aren't like house walls with air space."

The Jeulatong is very light-colored and brightens small cabins immensely.

"I agree with you about cutting old growth," I tell Baden in a whisper, glancing around for Peter. "Although our leader is quite fond of telling you what all of us think categorically, believe it or not, I have my own mind."

"Naaahhhhh. ..." says Baden in mock amazement.

"Yeah. I think that certain, carefully selected old growth trees should be allowed to be cut under strict guidelines for specific purposes, such as for wooden boat building and making fine instruments. But that's not what the purists believe." I pretend to search for hidden microphones under the wooden seat. "However, here in Canada old growth wood is still used for two-by-fours, and that's a crime."

Baden winces with pain as if his own limbs were being sliced.

"Up in the old growth taiga," I tell him, "where trees ten inches in diameter can be a hundred years old, they have put up pulp mills. The trees won't grow back, since there is almost no soil. Old growth is sacred," I conclude. "That is that."

Baden gleams. He feels vindicated from Peter's wrath. He has found a coconspirator. "I'm working to set up this network of fine craftsmen all over southwestern B.C. to support the idea of allowing old growth wood to be used for boat building. We thought we would have to fight environmentalists as well as the industry!"

I reassure him, saying, "To win protection for the forest, environmentalists have to form alliances with the wood worker, the fine craftsman, and the small mill owner. We must work together and increase labor-intensive wood industries. I don't believe that any cut-and-dried, absolute policy is going to work. ..."

I stop short. We'd hit a wall of white.

The solid bank of advection fog instantly grows so thick that we go from bright sunlight to air sodden enough to squeeze. "Advection fog forms," says Baden apprehensively, "when warm air from the Pacific hits upwelling cold water from below. The vapor condenses to form the most serious block to travel on this part of the planet. Stop talking." He snaps into his captain's alertness. Our thoughts blot out. I can barely see Baden, though he is only three feet away.

I am startled. Instantly my dry hair is sopping wet. All surfaces on the boat are beaded with swelling water drops. My black notebook pages swell and curl, then won't take ink.

Pouring over Baden's weather and sailing manuals, I discover that there are a number of causes for advection fog along this coast, but the most common is the sudden cooling of warm air that is moving horizontally over ocean water. When the air is cooled, the water it holds condenses into fog. The ocean here is complexly layered; one of the contributors is the Japanese ocean current, called the Kuroshio,[1] which brings warm water pouring over the cold, upwelling ocean.

Suddenly the blue-gray infinite, sloshing monotone of the ocean takes on a new character: one of multiple, complex chords rising from endless chaos to create a beautiful order.

Cold water upwelling through the Kuroshio also means lush marine life in the summer. Well fed by the thousands of rivers flowing down from the interior, which fill it with detritus and nutrition, the warm current mixes the river water with the cold upwellings of the benthic zone, which are full of dead flora and fauna, releasing proteins and minerals back into forms available for new life. The resultant complexity—land detritus as well as benthic nutrients mixing in warm water—is an incredible smorgasbord for life.

Though I hadn't experienced advection fog on the water before, I had experienced it on land. As the northwesterly airstream moves onshore and upslope, it produces extensive fog banks along the outer coast from Alaska to San Francisco. Once, driving in the Cascade Foothills, I was nearly blinded by advection fog, only to pop into sunlight in the space of forty seconds, after driving only seven hundred feet higher. When I turned to gaze back toward the coast, I found a striking cloud formation. In voluminous waves from miles out to sea,

---

[1] Kuroshio is derived from Kuro, meaning black, and shio, meaning tide. The Kuroshio circles up past Japan and eastward through Alaska, carving off small currents that curl counterclockwise, such as the current in Prince William Sound. It then continues down the coast of British Columbia and the United States.

the clouds scrolled over on themselves, mimicking ocean breakers—only in slow motion. In an hour, they were gone.

This advection fog bears a disturbing resemblance to the morning I spent in a Yukon whiteout high on the Arctic Circle, although that snow cloud was of an entirely differently origin. I take comfort in the idea that we will soon pop out of narrow Darby Channel, where barely submerged rocks threaten us. A metal marker in the middle of the channel delineates the only route through a narrow slot. The tension on the boat is thick enough to caulk floor tiles. After what seems like hours, we break free of the channel and are sailing through the open sea toward our next unexplored rain forest, the Hecate Lowlands.

When a slant of sun strikes through the fog, I can see that Baden is gazing intently out to sea, smiling. His body is talking directly with the beautiful craft under his feet—created of multiple wood fibers and pure spirit.

The Classic
Hecate Lowlands

Cape Caution, 50°48' N, 127°40' W
Miles Inlet, 50°40' N, 127°28' W

*T*oday the sea acts like the biceps of an underworld god doing push-ups. It tips our boat steeply up, then down, creating in my own muscles the very sinews of a living planet.

We are rounding Cape Caution, an outreach of mainland unprotected from the open ocean by outer islands. I ride on the bow of the ship leaning into the sea, squinting toward the lowland mounds ahead, each dimmer than the last in the fog, watching for the first hints of our particular landfall.

This is my first exposure to open ocean on a small craft. Huge Pacific swells gain momentum from far out at sea. Seeking protection from the ten-foot billows, we hurry toward the coast. On my high perch, I find these translucent green swells glorious—I could ride them forever. They are what is left of an open Pacific storm, its fury coalesced into steep swells rolling smoothly to greet the land in rhythmic susurrations. As the ocean bottom rises only a wave length in depth, the wave crests lean forward, grow monstrous with foam, and cover the shore with white froth.

A groaning, white-humped landmass emerges from the fog—long, low bedrock islands. Such islands represent the earliest soggy ecological communities to rise out of the sea on this part of the coast. The Hecate Lowlands are a land of emerging bogs and forests reinventing themselves. Even a mile away from the islands, we can see the hori-

99

zontal stripes of their various plant communities, the species determined by the tide levels. On the island tops, charcoal bands of stunted trees run like Mohawk haircuts. Below them, hundreds of cormorants dry their Machiavellian wings—jet-black Batman emblems against the gleaming guano rock. Below them, black lichen, barnacles, rockweed, and other colorful algaes begin their layered tapestries. Behind these first low islands, a bank of glowing fog hides the mainland's reality.

I feel estranged, wishing I could get away by myself. Cindy is wise, Baden kind, and Karen and Ian are a blast but still I feel like the token Ugly American. I thought the hard part of being a new sailor would be seasickness, but I have experienced absolutely not a trace. It is proximity that troubles me. I try to imagine what Joseph Conrad would do. He would write about it, of course.

Closer and closer to the mainland coast we draw, yet still no opening appears. I worry: How will we ever make it through these pounding waves? Centuries of shipwrecks sail through my mind; the west coast of Vancouver Island is full of sunken history. I wonder if they will write a folk song about us as lovely as the one about Lord Franklin's disappearance.

No glimpse of any entrance. Still we sail closer to the coast on the rougher and rougher water. This might be our inlet ... maybe not.

Abruptly the fog reveals a narrow opening; terra firma has opened herself to yet another boat of bedraggled sailors, and I am experiencing a new sort of vulnerability—a profound fear of being dashed into the rocks by the giant breakers.

The horrendous roar of the waves vised against the sides of the narrow channel now reaches our ears. This is Miles Inlet, tucked a short way into the west side of Bramham Island. Are we to enter here through these rapids? We slide shoreward with ease, catching smaller and smaller swells until we reach a quiet inlet with steep rock sides. Here, the extreme, seventeen-foot-high tides could easily swing our boat around. We must take care to anchor in deep enough water and tie to the shore in three places.

Karen and Ian's Zodiac takes me to a high rock near pools where otters play. How I savor the solitude of these wilderness fjords. Chanterelle mushrooms on the bank surge up out of the ground so thickly that they appear to be a cast-off, yellowing mattress in the alder. All around us, pools swell with the incoming tide. Multitudes of tiny fish leap. The tide's flow creates nets of tan bubbles that build up to fifteen inches high and jiggle in piles of dirty chiffon.

The sky, which has held its overcast vigil all day, opens up eggshell blue. In the sunlight I can see the zone system created by the layers of life: low tide, mesotidal, high tide, splash zone, and up to the red bog overdraped with contorted juniper and madrona.

On the spherical boulder where I sit, I am dreamily sinking into my own thoughts when Peter's small Zodiac buzzes up.

"Ian and Karen are off exploring, Cindy and Baden are taking care of the boat, so you're it. I need crew."

For an hour, we wander through T-shaped waterways formed in a perpendicular grid of miniature fault lines. From the impact of two tectonic plates crashing together, rocks crumbled in lines parallel to and perpendicular to the Pacific Plate. This odd criss-cross of secretive channels reveals treasures at each turn. In one, we accidentally flush nesting red-throated loons. A double surprise—we do not expect them here, let alone reproducing, because our bird guides all report their nest sites further north. These loons have never before been recorded as nesting here.

But then, practically nothing has been recorded here. To our knowledge, no amateur naturalist or scientist has made a systematic observation of the area. We could find no botanical lists categorizing the plants living here. The beauty of the area makes me yearn to sit here and observe for all of next summer!

Red-throated loons, *Gavia stellata*, are chortling in that wavering, primordial gargle that indicates fear. I hate to intrude on their nursery. This circumpolar diving bird breeds only in the Arctic and subarctic, or so my field guides tell me. If this is new nesting territory, it is important to inform the outside world. Their up-tilted bills and striking red necks surrounded by delicate, parallel lines lend the loons an air of lordship—perhaps they believe that humans won't dare take their fish, woods, and miniature fjord kingdom from them.

At each intersection of the grid, a miniature lagoon supports abundant life. Crabs dance on the rocks waving their claws at our disturbance. A primitive sculpin that has crawled out of the water lies gasping in a crack. Barnacles and slippery algae cover every inch of the pink granite. Wind-contorted junipers lean down over us, their roots eight feet above our heads. The flat bottom branches provide a measure of the highest of high tide.

Musing, I think that my talents would be better utilized by recording the bog ecology than by serving as a paddle-lackey for a video camera mobilization unit. Soon the channel is too shallow to paddle, so I must pole. Peter finds my skills as a poler so lacking (I am jerking the boat about with short thrusts) that I easily convince him to drop me off in the bog forest of one of the islands. Sort of like Bre'r Rabbit tricking Bre'r Fox into dropping him off in a briar patch for punishment. As I slip and slop my way up the rock in sneakers, I hear Peter say, "You're going to hate it up there—all buggy and boggy— *nothing* of interest. You'll get your butt wet!"

"Promise?" I yell back over the noise of the outboard motor.

At last, I am alone in a true bog forest within British Columbia's Hecate Lowlands. The boglands reinvent life on the islands in the slim, protected waterways that penetrate thirty miles up into the Fjordlands and Coast Range.

I am thrilled. The bogs are a veritable bank vault of vegetable investment laid down over one to four thousand years. Although no scientist has sampled the bogs' bottoms so far, I guess that boglands began to form soon after the last Ice Age and the postglacial rise in sea level.

To better know our own rain forest, it would help to know if these particular bogs were three thousand or nine thousand or merely several hundred years old. They would offer a clue to the length of time it takes for a mature forest ecosystem to develop to its full complexity.

With such concrete numbers, perhaps the timber extraction industry wouldn't slaughter these Hecate Lowlands with such impunity.

At last, face to face with the clandestine beginnings of the giant rain forest of North America, I become a time-giant watching ecosystems unfold. This shoreline is glacier-scraped bedrock, hostile to any forest. Yet here, within the bogs-becoming-soil, I can spin through the time spiral of a strange new planet without the aid of the Starship Enterprise.

Sloshing waves gulp unpleasantly close to me on the bulbous stone shore. Adjusting my large day pack full of guidebooks and equipment, I plunge into the gnarled tree of the bog forest, glancing about for trolls. Too much Hans Christian Andersen as a kid. Swallowed by stunted trees and calf-deep mosses, I lean back to contemplate the canopy's trapezoids of sky. Osprey, eagle, and loon wing by. At night black bear, marten, fisher, river otter, wolf, and mountain lion will vary their nutrition with shore and bog life.

I understand Peter's attitude about entering the stunted forest. Humans have long found bogs haunting and dreary. Peat moss's intriguing habit of swallowing mammoths, plows, hunters, and musk ox whole has made us afraid of bogs since our human beginnings. Because their acidity and lack of oxygen stops decay, bogs preserve the bodies of beast and man very well, an archaeologist's delight.

And they are power spots—for me.

I drop to my knees, take out a hand lens, then lie on my side in the soggy moss. From here, I can see a myriad, a veritable forest, of plants. The lens shrinks me to the size of a gnat, and I sail through thousands of minute, spongy star bursts ranging from deep red to bright orange to kelly green. Of the over three hundred sphagnum moss species thus far named, this bog harbors a dozen or more. Some are designed to stay submerged, while other pile up into pulvinate cushions fourteen inches high. These cushions, stuffed with their own dead brethren, are easy to kneel on. More important for the life of the bog, they allow shrub seeds to germinate just above the acidic-poisoned bog water. Since there is little bacteria or fungi present to attack these seeds, they may lie dormant for thirty years, then burst into life when the moss dries out just enough. Yet the Bog God can easily drown them again by raising the water level: creating another layer of dead vegetation to become soil for future trees.

Sphagnum, or peat moss, species are equipped with gas-filled cells that float, making them ingeniously adapted for immersion in water. Because of these cells, the plants are also able to remain unharmed by desiccation in dry seasons, or when crushed by snow, or when swollen by freezing water. The gas-filled sacks squeeze under my knees, causing me to feel a pleasant queasiness, like I get from holding a slug.

Above water, each gas-filled cell takes in air through a tiny pore. Underwater, the peat moss, which can hold two hundred times its own weight, acts like a sponge. When dead, the peat moss sinks into the water and weighs down older sphagnum moss deep in the bog, adding thickness to the floating, living plant. Slowly the plant spreads out over a water-filled depression until it roofs over the entire pond and mimics solid ground.

The dead moss rots slowly here. As it decomposes, it releases tannin and acid, which poison the very bacteria needed for the decay that recycles organic growth. Even its rich, nitrogenous parts are unavailable to bacteria that need oxygen to grow. Dead moss gathers for thousands of years until it is many feet thick and insulates the water below in relative warmth. Stained with tannin from the dying plants, the bog water becomes a dark, rusty brown to black.

Accidentally I sink in up to my upper thighs in a bog at the center of the small island. I plunge outward through its concentric circles of successive growth stages, from open water to forest. My movement is hard on the bog plants, but they *were* impersonating solid ground. Because these bogs form on scraped-out bedrock and are relatively shallow, I am not afraid of being swallowed. Escaping from the sphagnum moss, I move through a zone of shrubs that cling to the floating debris and moss and then, finally, onto something like soil. I finally reach a *strand*, a plant-made ridge of drier ground club moss and translucent, one-cell-thin tissue paper moss, *Hookeria lucens,* and goldenthread.

Sinking again ankle-deep, I slog through Labrador tea and bog rosemary, plants that indicate wet, nitrogen-poor soil and no water drainage. The dry ridge of bunchberries and false lilies of the valley that I come to next makes me believe that the nearby blooms of loosestrife are on solid ground.

Indeed, soon I am staggering up onto drier ground, exchanging fins for legs and gas bladders for lungs. Terra firma—I grow cocky. Shrubby plants spring from the mossy mat: bog blueberry, cranberry, red huckleberry, and salal. Deer fern add their delicate arches over red and purple liverworts, and bracken fronds vault overhead. Up on higher ground, western juniper and Sitka spruce branches drip with twenty-foot strands of *Alectoria vancouverensis,* a lichen endemic to these shores. Shaggy-barked yew trees grow full of the chemical compound taxol, which, scientists have found counteracts breast cancer.

In this magical forest full of bright berries and treasures, I am strolling around upright, admiring my clever cognitive capacity. Then—sploosh—I de-evolve into a floundering being again.

I've shocked myself by stepping onto another "solid ground" ruse: a soggy moss mat that is buoyant enough to hold my weight, as well as that of an entire thicket of woody plants. The roots twist around floating plants, knitting the bog forest together. Until I can extricate myself from this delicate root tangle, I rock on a mossy waterbed, causing trees fifty feet away to tilt crazily.

Finally, there is enough dry earth for me to sink my butt down into layers of soft club moss. Tilting back, I contemplate the dripping epiphytes in this unearthly, spectral world.

In Praise of Orchids

A raven unwinds his deep-pitched *kerrronk* twelve feet overhead. All is right with my world. I am lying on my side to write when I become aware of a pale apparition before my eyes. Pulling back, I discover a most beautiful, inverted inflorescence, which hovers like a vegetative Lazarus above the dark crowberry mat. The miniature off-white blooms of the Rein orchid, *Habenaria orbiculata*, hang upside down on a slowly spiraling raceme. These orchids, which have evolved with the bogs, have thrived by being very unplantlike. Seeming to harken back to earlier plant forms, they do not depend upon their own photosynthesis but instead draw nutrients from tree roots.

Because orchids' root fungi prefer acidic soil, they are the quintessential bog bloom. I rise and wander in search of more.

I stumble next upon *Habenaria dilatata*, the white bog orchid. Eerily incandescent in the gloom, it seems to be powered by the flow of ancient bog souls. Then I spy the twayblade, whose minute purple-brown blooms hover above two roundly connected leaves like a sword's hasp on each stem. I remember the shock I felt each time I found the tropical-pink calypso orchids in the deep North Cascades forest. I am in the land of orchids.

These bogs are "orchid-stral" stages, botanical symphonies of strange adaptations, a synthesis of old and new, counterpoints of evolutionary successes and failures. Humans find orchids provocative, perhaps because they sense that, like mushrooms, these plants dance symbiotically with fungi and living trees. Living vicariously from others' photosynthesis rather than directly from sunlight, they have ghostly, fleshy hues. Freed from the necessity of green, their asymmetical blooms pout with exaggerated lower lips, which serve as landing pads for their symbiotic insect pollinators.

A little higher in the coastal forest, I come across coral root, *Corallorhiza* ssp., which has no chlorophyll-green parts or visible leaves. One singular coral root's foot-tall, fleshy-red spike will suddenly stand out, and then many will appear. These epiparasites rise like fleshy fingers from the forest floor. How did these and other orchids seduce the green plants and mycorrhizal fungi, somehow convincing the whole system to supply them with carbohydrates and minerals?

We do not know what, other than charm, they give back to the plant. With other plants working for them, the orchids, in a daring de-evolution, got rid of their own roots and now retain only vestigial leaves. Next they'll sprout legs and gallop off toward Peterson's *Field Guide to Western Mammals*.

For years, people could not grow orchids from seeds. We did not know that orchids use obligatory symbiotic mycorrhizae at their roots in a manner that is unique among plants. Then, in 1904, French botanist Noel Bernard discovered that orchid seeds need to be infected with various fungi in order for them to germinate. The seeds, so tiny that many can fit on the head of a pin, cannot carry enough nutrients to sustain themselves or the tiny seedlings that sprout from them; it is the fungi that supply the needed food. The root fungi does not stop helping after germination, but spreads a fine web of fungal filaments that help the orchid develop shoots for carrying on its own photosynthesis. Many of the twenty-five thousand known orchid species, such as the tropical forest lianas, develop no roots at all but live off air and moisture. Several species are old growth forest indicators, since it takes many years for the correct symbiotic mycorrhizae to establish themselves in the soil.

Such amazing three- or four-way symbioses, involving plants, insects, mycorrhizae, and trees, seem to represent a process of turning separate organisms into one. Reminiscent of the first eukaryotic cells, which formed when simpler cells surrounded and incorporated the functions of other cells, could orchids be turning into new beings in these bogs? Not really, but it is an entertaining thought.

On earth, prokaryotic organisms, single cells without a nucleus, far predated the more complex eukaryotic cells. Eukaryotic cells have nuclei and a variety of organelles that can serve different functions. Their formation enabled life to leap forward into more complex organisms.

Lynn Margulis, whose breakthrough discovery (as yet unprovable) that a symbiosis between earlier organisms enabled such an evolutionary leap, believes that another billion years would have been required for the slow evolution of prokaryotic cells to invent nuclei and the other assets that enabled life to progress. She used circumstantial fossil evidence to suggest that symbiosis of several prokaryotic organisms created new life. By examining the various DNAs of different organisms, she found that the mitochondria, flagella, cilia, and photosynthetic plastids within cells often seemed to have originated from separate organisms.

From this research, Margulis formed an elegant theory called endosymbiosis. In endosymbiosis, separate species work together so well and for so long that they actually become one organism. Margulis found concrete evidence that, in our wildest imaginings, leads to the Gaia theory.[1] The Gaia theory says simply that since all life on earth evolved together, much of it in symbiosis, the entire life of all five kingdoms along with the rock mantle and oxygenated atmosphere of Earth function as one huge, interrelated being: the biosphere.

These Hecate Lowlands absolutely enthrall me. Everything works together—I can watch the forest trying to begin on the swaying moss mat. The orchids' extensive symbiosis is stunning. Paleobotanists conjecture that plant life was able to climb out of the sea due to a symbiosis between marine algae and fungi. Plant roots were fossilized with mutually beneficial mycorrhizae four hundred million years ago. The orchids seem to parallel this history.

Watching life coat bare rock, I realize that life did not form and then move forward in a simple growth curve. Life is constantly stopping, starting, jumping, and reinventing itself. I think about all the pervasive, even global, demolitions, the periodic and demonic wipeouts such as took place at the end of the Cretaceous period.

---

[1] Nicolette Perry, *Symbiosis: Close Encounters of the Natural Kind* (Dorset, U.K.: Blandford Press, 1983), 12.

Life buries, hides, dissolves, whistles, roars, devours, and buzzes itself into being right in front of my eyes. Right now, here in this very bog, I am a momentary grace note in life's intricate music. Next waltz around, I may not even be asked to dance.

Part Three

The Lost Continent of Cascadia

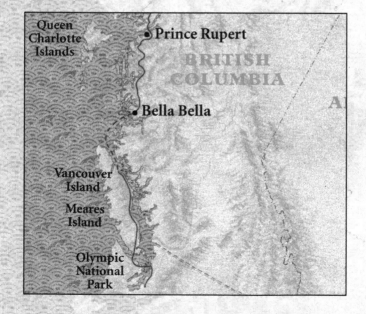

Introduction

50°52'36" N × 128°25'51" W
48°18'33" N × 123°15'49" W

A mediocre nightclub singer with thick mascara, glittering eye shadow, and pink cheeks moans out urban blues from a culture alien to her own. Trembling florescent lights turn human faces a submerged yellow as they chatter with one another at dime-sized plastic tables. Everything inside this ship is designed to cut one off from the rainy, cold outside world. The *Queen of the North* sets me down gingerly in Port Hardy on north Vancouver Island. It is after midnight. I have abandoned my five Canadian friends in Bella Bella, picked up Die Fledermazda, and now feel expanding freedom.

The ferry has docked on a vestigial fragment of an exotic terrane[1] that floated in from the west in recent geological time, two hundred million to fifty million years ago. This mysterious continent, called Cascadia, joined and then disconnected from the mainland, rising and falling into the ocean, four different times. On each submergence, it gathered limestone mumbling with fish, shells, trilobites, amphibians, and reptiles. As the sea level bounced up and down with the lockup of water during the Ice Ages, Cascadia's umbilical cord to the continent was cut and rejoined. When the waters rose around Cascadia most recently, it left the two-hundred-mile-long fragment that white settlers called Vancouver Island.

---

[1] A terrane is a geologic term for a landform of homogeneous origin or rock type.

The land bridge jutting north and northeast from Cape Scott to the mainland appeared and disappeared like the Cheshire cat. All that remains now is a grin, fifty miles of treacherous islands, rock piles, and strange currents. If the *Queen of the North* had only arrived a bit sooner, say thirty thousand years sooner, we could have seen pygmy horses and camels, musk ox wallowing in peat, New World rhinoceroses, wooly mammoths, and even monkeys before they packed their bags for Asia. It is to Cape Scott's peninsula and chain of islands that I long to go—a half-day's drive and two days' backpack north.

A great wild edge, this northern shore. Named by Captains Lawrie and Guise in 1786 for Captain David Scott, a Bombay merchant, the water off the Cape Scott shore swallows ships whole. On November 15, 1860, the *American Consort* and on March 24, 1892, the *Henry Davis* cracked up on an entry reef to San Josef's Bay. Early in this century, a lighthouse was erected on the triangular island twenty-five miles to the west. It was soon abandoned, however, and its wireless station dismantled and rebuilt elsewhere. A new lighthouse built in 1960 continues today to pulse through the deep fog that envelops this inhospitable land.

Because Cascadia consisted of young, rugged mountains, its submerged remains along Vancouver Island's 715-mile-long perimeter are squirrelly and complex. The north and west coasts are notched with deep inlets and bays, channels and haystacks, roaring currents and hidden reefs, that are notorious for causing disasters and failed communities. Mountains rise straight up out of the churning waves—no beach, no pause, no transition.

Storms still make travel for most craft along the north and west coasts almost impossible in winter. Powerful Pacific weather systems can churn up waves a hundred feet high. The surging waters, zero visibility, and, dangerous cliffs make for lonely shores. Between Cape Scott and Quatsino Inlet forty miles to the south, the coast has long been devoid of human dwellings.

The Wide Bights
of Cape Scott

50°35' N, 128°15' W

The folks of Port Hardy try their best to discourage me. "You hafta drive up a really rough logging road forty or fifty miles to San Josef's Camp. There it ends, and you can't drive no further," a native declares.

I say confidently, "I will backpack out to an extreme point of land."

The man continues, "There ain't much up there. The oldest white settlement on the island, Quatsino, Scandinavian, was abandoned. Pretty depressing. Port Alice has a population of five hundred souls and a pulp mill, but that ain't near where you're going."

Another man tells me, "At the end of Holberg Inlet, there is one garage, one post office, one restaurant, and the logging camp headquarters." With a twinkle in his eye he adds, "That's the industry that you can thank for leveling the northern end of the island."

I gas up and go.

About ten miles in, hundreds of shoes are nailed to a hundred foot cedar. No explanation. Just a sign reading "SHOE TREE."

Twenty miles in, a huge tree lies crushing an early-1960s rocket-finned car flat to the ground. I chuckle until I realize some young guy really loved this car, a real cruiser. On top is a large sign that reads "EXPECT THE UNEXPECTED."

Next I see a sign depicting a series of red elephants crossing the road, trunk in tail, wittily suggesting behemoth traffic ahead. Soon a system of green, yellow, and red circles begins indicating on which roads one may travel, on which roads one can maybe travel, and on which roads one will die. It's a good system.

I have been driving through the ninety percent of British Columbia that is public land "managed" by the Ministry of Forests for private industry. In 1955, the provincial government began granting long-term tree farm licenses to private companies, providing them with unlimited and exclusive cutting rights. The deals were fraught with bribes. Deforestation in British Columbia soon outpaced the liquidation of forests in all of the United States and equaled that of Brazil during its worst clearcutting period.

Due to a lack of national environmental laws, such as the United States' Endangered Species Act, logging in British Columbia was essentially unregulated. Those regulations that were in place were written by the logging industry itself with the sanction of the Forest Service. Very little enforcement was available: In 1989 there were only forty-three Forest Service employees, all stationed in Port Alberni, for all of three-hundred-mile-long Vancouver Island. To make matters worse, the staff included no hydrologists, soil scientists, or wildlife biologists. Consequently, the forests sheltering the region's fisheries and vital wildlife harbors—such as Shark River, where sharks give birth under waterfalls—were recklessly cut. Above Robson Bight, home of the largest gathering of orca whales on Earth, the Tsitika Watershed was partially cut. Those private citizens who complained because their lives were being ruined as their surrounding livelihood and scenic views disappeared were slapped with lawsuits by large multinational industries for blocking an industry's right to make a fortune.

[Author's update: There is hope. By 1999, at the writing of this book, cutting has been greatly slowed in British Columbia, and panels made up of government scientists, industry, and aboriginal groups have been meeting to find alternatives to clearcutting. Reflecting the changing trends, in January 1999, the Honorable Sheila Copps, federal minister of Canadian heritage, announced that the Canadian government has submitted an application for a Biosphere Reserve solution for Clayoquot Sound. By June, it may be a reality. Clayoquot Sound is one of the last and largest relatively intact temperate rain forest watershed in North America and the center of great logging controversy.

Since 1972 when Pacific Rim National Park was established, millions of international visitors have fallen in love with the immense forests of Vancouver Island. Many were dismayed by the April 13, 1993, announcement by the B.C. government that it would cut two thirds of Clayoquot Sound. Even more disturbing was that old growth forest liquidation on the island reached record levels that year; the timber industry could see regulation coming and wanted to cut before cutting was curtailed. People from all over the world hiking the Pacific Rim National Park's West Coast Trail could hear the chain saws just a mile away as they walked the "wilderness." Surfers were shocked as they found the land adjacent to their beaches cut right down to the water. Twelve thousand people gathered to hold the largest protest in Canadian history, peacefully blocking the loggers at the Kennedy River Bridge. Nine hundred of the protesters were arrested. As the logging continued, worldwide campaigns were initiated to point out consumer complicity in the purchase of wood products from such clearcuts. The efforts resulted in huge boycotts by European companies such as Der Spiegel, a publishing house, and Scott Paper of Europe. Today, boycotts of British Columbian old growth lumber by U.S. companies are very effective.

By February 1994, forestry practices had greatly improved. Under international pressure, the provincial government passed some tough new forest protection laws. Clearcutting is now against the law and enforced by fines of up to $1.5 million per violation, and the granting of new tree farm licenses is conditional, based on the company's previous forestry practices. The new selective logging that will replace clearcutting is being allowed over an even greater area of British Columbia than the intensive cutting was before, but huge, protected wilderness areas have been proposed.]

∽

I receive a mental bruising as I gaze at the wide clearcuts, the destroyed streams, and the land slumping off entire mountainsides revealing bare rock. Only night soothes me. My sight is limited to an eery tunnel of headlight that flickers off the immense trunks of ancient trees.

In the morning, I am delighted to find I have entered a magnificent grove of old growth—giant Douglas fir, hemlock, and western red cedars that were left by the timber industry for campers. The bases of these trees loom as wide as my long-bed pickup is long. I stretch and climb out into a wondrous, trollish-tale world. I point my face upward and sway in all directions to catch a glimpse of the trees' tops, but they disappear, spiraling into the canopy. The industry's foresters call these grand old individuals "overripe," yet they have grown the greatest biomass per hectare (2.47 acres) on the planet, more massive than in equatorial rain forests.

Ten-foot-wide trees. I am but a mouse dwarfed by the giants. The forest floor is wide and open, covered by a thick layer of aromatic needles through which pop twelve-inch-wide, warning-sign-yellow amanitas. Their white-spotted tops, the dark tree columns, and the angular slants of sun make a Walt Disney magical forest dim in comparison.

Here, enough time has passed since the last wipeout of trees by ice for the forests to have aged and fallen back into the earth several times. The current hemlock forest towers. The "overmature" cedar monsters lean in what the logging industry calls "decline," yet it is a stage that produces abundant new life as the trees fall both on top of the nurse logs and on the small patches of sunlit floor. There is no permanent death in the cycles of forest. Dead trees become nurse logs even before they fall, sprouting new hemlocks and many shrubs along their lengths. Walking through these silent forests, I am struck by enormous hemlocks that grow in perfectly aligned, numinous corridors. A Parthenon of grace, it seems an invisible architect works within the cycles of life and death.

After hiking all day, I crawl into the back of my pickup to sleep, leaving the tailgate open. The night noises build to a crescendo with the croaks of countless frogs, the soft hoots of owls, the quavering calls of loons. I can barely sleep in anticipation of what tomorrow will bring. In the morning I will backpack out onto the rugged spine and hike clear to the north end of Cascadia. My ancestral genes from Land's End, the southern rocky tip of the British Isles, are driving me to the farthest reach of Vancouver Island.

Thick fog stuck to the ground when I started out at 8:00 A.M. This forest always drips—even when the sky is clear. The mist now rolls up in skeins or winds up through the canopy in blurry shawls. These venerable woods are clearly a continuation of those in the Hecate Lowland bogs. The difference is that they have had a few hundred more years to weave their ecosystem. An uneven canopy sieves the sun, so few shrubs survive on the wide, open forest floor. Beneath each hemlock, seventy million needles crunch underfoot. The trees' fallen twigs bounce as if on mattress springs. Far above, the canopy, entangled with epiphytes and long strands of lichen, grows a second forest floor as thick as thatched roofs in England.

Floors upon roofs upon floors upon roofs.

Notre Dame shafts of viridescent light slant down through giant Sitka spruce. From my perspective on the ground, the thriving canopy species seem to hide. In Carmanah Valley, on the west coast Vancouver Island, scientist Neville Winchester discovered hundreds of species as yet unknown to science in one canopy station alone. (Loggers retaliated by destroying the canopy stations that were built with great difficulty high in the trees, but that is another story.)

Now, feeling the elixir of solitude, I am wading a waterlogged trail to Cape Scott. A frog crosses my boot—a good sign in this time of the disappearance of frogs all over the world. In a wilderness so lugubrious and lovely at the same time, I happily anticipate five days of total immersion.

But solitary I am not. The forest is filled with life. I am painfully aware that my inadequate senses set me apart. Haptic moles move under me feeling their burrows, epiphytes filter sun rays above; all green breathing surfaces expand and contract.

An exhalation of leaves; an exaltation of trees.

I plunge down an abandoned trail.[1] My boots slip past puzzling holes in the humus with archways of moss, fern, and skunk cabbage. The smell of ancient bedclothes and earth wafts up. I can hear vague trickles through loose, underground stone passages, while racemes of white blooms vibrate on the ground above.

Old Kelty pack strapped in place, I travel like a forest-green hunchback through dark tunnels, through boreal labyrinths.

Decayed bridges made of cedar logs span two thirty-foot-deep channels of brackish water. The first one I am able to negotiate on its plankless stringers[2] by holding onto young hemlock branches. At the second, I must either turn back or do an impossible balancing act to make it over the one slick support log left. All of the planks and the other supports are gone. I get down on my hands and knees to distribute my weight and lower my center of gravity. Beneath me a tumble of cedar logs and prickly devil's club leaves stare longingly at my flesh. I hope nobody will witness me leaving my human form behind.

On the far side, the trail shoots fifty feet straight up a steep-sided gully, then down into the San Josef River drainage. Negotiating fallen six-foot-thick logs slick with wet moss and surfaces polished by the endless rain requires the modus operandi of a slug.

My hands and feet become separate animals with minds of their own as I scurry through the roots and branches and up the mud canyons. This is the magical point when backpackers transform into forest animals. Struggling up and down mud canyons, grasping red slippery roots as handles, my mind becomes secondary, drops from awareness. I am all instinct, kinesthetics, sniffing.

---

[1] A new boardwalk has since been completed, with the trail rerouted, so that it is an easy walk to the Scandinavian ghost village of Cape Scott.

[2] Stringers are the rough-stripped poles, usually nine to twelve inches in diameter, that support trail and bridge planks through the soggy rain forests.

A voice in my brain shifts from willful past and future tenses to immersion in the present.

Hiking on a trail of rotten cedar planks, it takes me two and a half hours to go the remaining five miles to camp. Old mud ruts, once wagon roads, lead to failed Danish farms. Support beams over tiny creeks now sprout dwarf dogwood, moss and small hemlock, suspended rugs that cave in with grim regularity. Through slits in the furred bridges, I watch tannin water gurgling away to the ocean.

As the tall forest gives way to a bog, the trail rambles through a grove of contorted shore pine that look like Bonsai. Where cedar planks won't hold, human feet have created deep, black mud holes. In some, I sink to my knees. In one, I sink up to my thigh and have trouble extricating my foot with the boot still on it. The hundreds of humans have widened the trail not out of carelessness but because this is the only way to maneuver.

As my boot heels slice down a gully, I notice there is almost no soil. Humus only half an inch thick covers impervious clay. Soils under much of the rain forest are poor in quality. The organic capital is stored in the trunks, mycorrhizae, epiphytes, and canopy. For twelve thousand years, rich organic investment has been deposited up in the air, not in the ground. The forest industry's claims that the great trees will grow back quickly are simply not biologically possible. Instead, the industry is quickly eradicating the island's botanical wealth while silting the streams and eliminating wildlife corridors. When trees are clearcut, the island is left covered with only thin, slumping clay on bedrock.

Because fog completely engulfs the trail, I stumble, unaware, upon the village of Cape Scott. What all backpackers seek: the sense of discovery.

Almost nothing remains of the school, the dance hall, the large dairy farm abandoned in 1956. Dairy cows once turned the lush marsh grass into cheese, meat, and milk, but the markets were too far away and the Inside Passage too dangerous to negotiate in winter. Nobody died on these farms except for the Christenson boy at age twelve. This was not a tragic site, merely an ill-conceived endeavor compounded with much hard labor.

From an ecological perspective, I always find something heartening about civilization in reverse. Here, the village buildings are entirely gone, repossessed by trees and land in just forty years. Roots tangle over dreams and devour machine parts. A bed frame leans inside a cedar bower. Two people probably made love here, if they had any energy left after working. An iron gate still stands, wired shut, with no fence. A doorknob hangs oddly suspended by a wire, but the door is long gone. A portal with no interior. A foundation that did not hold.

Out on the marsh, ghost cows graze. Their bells tinkle over the marsh the Danes stole back from the sea.

At the mouth of Fisherman's River, at the north end of the marsh, the Danes built a seven-foot-high dike with primitive tools in 1899–1900. The whole community planned to share collectively the wealth that would come pouring in from the enormously rich, diked bog meadows. But the day the dike was finished, a massive storm washed it out to sea.

Again they built, and this dike lasted a while longer—five years—until 1907. It was a backbreaking way to create land: not by stripping a forest but by borrowing it from the ocean. Danes had genetic memories for such skills. Now, as I cross the bog on board planks and a soggy trail, flowing, muddy channels are slowly taking the soil back to the sea. I thank those long-gone Danes whose private ownership and industry, ironically, kept this northern tip of the island from being logged.

Gazing toward the north end the marsh, I see a dark hole in the forest swallow the trail. I slog toward this forest opening and a half hour later, as I plunge into darkness, I feel the temperature plummet thirty degrees—no transition.

Before reaching the forest's outer edge, I can hear the white roar of the sea broken into rhythmic peaks and lulls. The forest tunnel spits me out on Nel's Bight, where it is hot. Across a graceful, three-mile-long curve of sand, translucent waves roll toward shore in lazy, turquoise arcs. The beach light stuns my eyes. Tired and sweaty under my pack, I keep walking until I find the potable tannin water at the west end of the beach. Drinking fully, I return to the center of the arc and sprawl, exhausted in the sand. As I doze off, layers of beach sounds—clacking stones, gentle waves, gurgles of sea birds—merge with the smells of salt water, cedar, and molding sea algae. Everything blurs together in an ancient knob at the top of my spine.

A great ruckus overhead awakens me rudely. Two bald eagles wrestle high in an old snag, squealing unabashedly. One fluffs out twice its size, enjoying the warmth of the sun. The other one sits and stares adoringly at its mate. Absolutely regal with huge yellow beaks, they still act goofy in love.

I sink back down onto the warm ground. Again I fall to sleep, only to be awakened by grand screeching. I open one eye a crack. The eagles, focusing out to sea, scream in disgust. No predator exists for them here; what could possibly be the matter?

A dot is enlarging far out in the sky. It expands into an osprey. As it nears the shore, it plunges feet first into the strait and rises, struggling, with a fifteen-pound salmon. It has a great deal of trouble rising, overdone its weight-lifting capacity. The eagles are pissed.

Then the osprey carries out a wonderful maneuver, flipping the salmon parallel to its direction of flight. This is no easy trick considering that the fish is greater in size and weight than the bird. The osprey carries it with one foot in front of the other by pivoting an opposing thumb talon around on a specially evolved hinge. Eagles cannot do this. Eagles hate show-offs.

Unable to sleep, I gaze out toward the last dorsal rock fin of Cascadia: the last Scott Island. The thin neck of sand that connects Cape Scott to the rest of Vancouver Island is but a few eagle wingspreads wide at high tide. Attaching and detaching, attaching and detaching—I sense the rhythm of continents and glaciers in this neck of land. The rhythm of eons.

I daydream of animals wandering over an isthmus of land for a pleasant day of picnicking only to find themselves stranded for the millennium. In an evolutionary process called island biogeography, the animals stranded on islands grow bigger and darker (in the north) until their DNA is distinct from that of their kin on the mainland. The genetic changes can be swift, spurred on by each variance in the annual weather pattern. Even one year of extreme weather will make a difference. Those animals that can survive aridity well do better one year: those that grow bigger and more elusive survive better the next.

Thus evolution is not a slow curve upward like the sales chart of a successful company. It is an endless series of oscillations, appearing chaotic at any given moment in geological time.

Bones of an ancient horse have been found on the older island of Cascadia, indicating survival here after horses had disappeared on the mainland. Later, this same branch of horse turned up in Asia, where they finished evolving into the modern horse. Giant beavers once trimmed these forests; on Texada Island in the Inside Passage, a large form of *aplodontia* still exists.

The grizzly never made it over the land bridge, but the black bear did. Birds and most bats arrived here by flight. No skunks or badgers made nooky on Vancouver Island, yet wolverines did. Surprisingly, the nearly ubiquitous coyote did not make it over, but the gray wolf has stared down the island's centuries with yellow eyes. The mountain lion made it, but not the bobcat. Lost in revery of how certain animals made it here from the mainland and others did not, I watch a crowd of harlequin ducks float by on a driftwood raft.

I wander out to the end of the cape. Here I have a vertiginous sensation, as if I am flying through space on a spinning ship. Zapping through space with a trailing electromagnetic aurora, like beautiful cobalt-purple scarves, I narrowly miss asteroids. My cheeks are burning. I feel as if I am on a thin green fur covering a strange planet, barely covered by a five-mile-thin skin of air. Sunlit molecules buzz my eyelids.

I feel as if I am flying through space on a one-of-a-kind ship unique to the universe. There is not another human being on the planet. There is not another planet vaguely like this for light years. A great feeling of safety comes over me. I am glued to this spinning ship like a limpet by an existential epoxy: symbiosis. I spread my arms and walk into the sea.

Meares Island,
Clayoquot Sound:
West Coast of Vancouver Island

48°40' N, 125°55' W

*T*he locals, chattering in easy familiarity, move from table to table, never exchanging greetings or taking a breath. The fabric of conversation is so tightly knotted in three dimensions that to catch any thread and pull is to lead through and tighten the minds and hearts of all.

This is not tourist season. I, the only stranger, have just ordered a cinnamon roll, which turns out to be the size of a buoy. This is the Tofino bakery, the intelligence, communication, and early-warning radar control center of the village. A small fishing village with a huge heart, Tofino lies on the north edge of Pacific Rim National Park on the edge of Clayoquot Sound.[1]

I have come with the express purpose of sleeping in an isolated island ecosystem, Meares Island. Home to twenty-two thousand acres of rare, original coastal rain forest, Meares Island is relatively untouched. Its trees have been altered only by the Opitsat natives, who have lived within them for thousands of years.

---

[1] Clayoquot Sound, the center of great forestry practice controversy in the early 1990s, remains, at the time of this writing, a relatively undemolished watershed on Vancouver Island.

I gaze absently out the window of the bakery at seaplanes that buzz like giant water bugs into the dock to park like family stationwagons. A child of five trips into the bakery and scoots in next to a grizzled, red-haired, red-cheeked fisherman. The child's angelic face stares lovingly up at the fisherman who is growling, "Only took four thousand tons of herring when I was expecting seventeen thousand. Where th' 'ell are th' fish!" It was one of those silted-up, rhetorical questions.

The child looks afraid, not understanding the content of his father's words but sensing their consequence.

"We are the real industries, fishing and tourism! The provincial government doesn't give a goddamn about us. They only recognize the big industries that line their pockets. Screw the fisherman!" snarls the fisherman.

"Screw the tourist industry. Screw the artist. Screw the tour guide," snarls the tour guide.

"Screw the Opitsat family. Screw the whale watching industry," says a weathered-skinned man with a long ponytail.

"Screw the cook!" says the sweet-faced young woman standing behind the counter.

❧

For one whose landlocked life has been far too deprived of boats, the slopping seawater in the harbor seems momentous. Yet, it is not unmomentous to those who make their living from it: the gnarled fisherman, the garrulous whale watch guide, the knackety dory commuter, the homestead-by-the-sea forester. Like new planets, they cool on the surface but remain boiling underneath.

I stare at the Paul Klee outside the window: the bright triangles and the vertical rhythm of masts on the steel gray soup. The rhythms of the sails, broken by the upside-down triangles of the float planes on the silver-gray water matrix.

Survival-suit-orange upright worms trudge up and down the steep plank, the tide far out, lugging their fishing gear. In late winter, the water is so cold that one has ten minutes after falling in before hypothermia is debilitating. Survival suits float humans like helium balloons in the steel soup.

ॐ

This is the morning that I am to leave for Meares, and the mist is so thick that I can set cooking pots in it. It *will* clear, I tell myself over and over, as if the sound of a human voice holds sway with the heavens. I am determined to spend the night on Meares Island and have arranged for one of the island's guardian angels to take me over. Yesterday, I explained my intention to a skeptical Vancouver Islander. The conversation was brief: "I want to know what the old growth forest *feels* and *sounds* like all night long," I said. The man I was speaking to leaned back with mockery in his sea-gray eyes and tapped the two-inch-thick polyurethane tabletop with shells in it, saying, "DRIP DRIP DRIP DRIP DRIP DRIP DRIP!"

ॐ

Sharon Palm climbs into her skiff on Strawberry Island, where she lives in a turn-of-the-century ferry that has been lofted up onto land and propped up with struts. Watching her from the other side of the harbor a quarter mile away, I start down the dock with a fifty-pound pack, three gallons of water, a lantern, and a lunch bag, to the great amusement of the locals. The plank is very steep. Near the bottom, whoosh, my Vibram soles sail out from under me. I crash down hard and get up with one smooth motion as if I had been intentionally trying to pick something up. Martha Graham would have envied the move.

Good God, the smell of sea water! The euphoria that comes to land-dwellers when they get close to the sea. An opaque mirror, the water surface holds such secrets beneath, such weird topographies.

I smell and smell and remember with the memory of ancestors dragging gear down to other seas off other mist-shrouded islands long ago.

The Pacific pries open my dead senses with a crowbar. So wet, so green, so rhythmic, so moldy. Fish-smelling, sloshing black water streaked with silver wind stripes. The underwater realm teams with krill and amphipods twitching in constant undulation, an arpeggio played by a billion moving feet. Transparent organisms, looking like cut-away engine diagrams, pulse under the sea, their stomachs pumping in simple tubes, their red veins visible, colored by a dash of Day-Glo orange for recognition.

To the Opitsat natives, human symbionts who have meshed with the forest and sea since before memory, home and nature are seamless. The Opitsat people traveled seasonally to harvest clam beds, to hunt whales in the spring, and to live at the mouths of rivers in winter. Prehistoric trails worn in the wrinkled brow of Meares Island trace their annual routes.

The totem pole carved by Opitsat native Joe David to protect Meares Island was so beautiful to white man's eyes that the British Columbian Provincial Museum purchased it. It now stands guard over a patch of Victoria near the parliamentary buildings where the Forest "Ministry" resides. The totem that now stands guard over Meares Island, Weeping Cedar Woman, was carved by a white man.

The island is named for Captain John Meares of England, who at first befriended, not slaughtered, the natives. Before Meares' arrival, English Captain Robert Gray sent his men to burn the Opitsat village to the ground after Chief Wickanninish attempted to capture his ship.[2] Not a stellar beginning.

Sharon Palm, an excellent natural historian of Meares Island, briefs me succinctly of its dangers. She is obviously concerned about this odd, lone woman writer camping there.

"Dangerous mudflats stretch for miles at low tides, so don't be enticed far out and get trapped by a rapidly returning tide. Even though we have been working on the trails for years now, they cause real con-

[2] Ruth Kirk, *Tradition and Change on the Northwest Coast* (Seattle: University of Washington Press, 1986), 212.

fusion. My husband and I feel the best way to protect Meares Island is to bring visitors from all over the world who will come to care about the land and write letters. But we've also been raising six children in a broken-down ferry with no running water, so it takes time."

To myself, I wonder how much wood must be cut to raise six children for eighteen years?

Sharon, examining my physique and funky, old equipment, continues: "You will be completely alone," she says with grave concern. "No one to call on in an emergency. The Opitsat village is fifty miles away on the north lobe of this horseshoe-shaped island."

"Not to worry," I reassure her boisterously. "I'm tough as a desert."

So here I crouch all alone in a creaking rain forest. All 126 inches of annual precipitation are focused on my head. As Sharon's orange worm suit in her silver shrimp hors d'oeuvre dish roared off, I almost leapt into the water after her. But there are such things as pride and decorum. The forest is as dark as a moonlit night although it is 10:00 A.M. The trees have knitted their hands together against my entrance.

I go immediately to work on survival in the pouring rain. Tying my army poncho to some tree branches, I shove all of my gear under it. Then I set up the tent, also under the poncho's protection. Next I turn my attention to making brisk movements to keep warm, and the trail obliges: Shooting immediately up over highly polished roots that gleam like marble cathedral steps traversed by centuries of Catholics, it is rigorous. Hiking with my head down in concentration, I run into huge canine excrement full of finger-sized bones. Wolf-sized excrement. Wolf-hungered. I have heard that a pack of wolves frequents this island, an easy swim from the mainland. Black bears also cover this island with berry-filled scat, but this scat is an immense tubular extrusion, not a pie-mound.

The "trail" is nothing at all like the trails of the Lower Forty-Eight, which have been engineered for the stumbling masses. It capitulates to every root form, every rock, every gully. It requires a climb and belly flop over a six-foot-diameter fallen log and then careful foot placement: The shining red cedar roots in the rain are as slick as margarine. A steep mud chute carries me down into the next drainage, my Vibram soles leaving perfect crenulated heal-swooshes. Next, I climb through a jungle gym of smaller roots, leap across a submerged log in a stream, fall short, fall in, and wade up the mud bank, my boots making vulgar sucking noises.

Avian mating ruckus spins off through the jungle and out on the mudflat, a creaking cacophony. A grating of gear. A wild cackle of schizophrenia. Grebes and buffleheads make aquatic love on the water. Ducks take off from the water surface with eggbeater wings. The trill of a plum-sized winter wren escapes from the brush. The wet-finger-round-wine-glass ring of varied thrush fills the air, a sustained note that epitomizes the rain forest.

I squat on the rocky mudflat. Positioned this low, I can watch a thousand geysers spurt up from clammy inhabitants expunging their water, filtering out the food.

Sheets of rain begin to pour down: cascades, waterfalls, and whole water beds sloosh down my back. I plunge back into the forest's dark interior to find Sharon's "Hanging Garden Tree," a remarkable old complexity that she claims I must see. Over one thousand years old, it is easy to find. Its forty-meter purée of live and dead limbs, roots, and hanging roots serve whatever function befits the position they find themselves in. The secret genetics of old growth hemlock can, as if by magic, recode a branch to be a root, or a branch to a trunk. If I were so versatile, I would grow a foot on my forehead, two hands on my elbows, and an eye in the back of my head.

Included in this tree collage, squirreled among the hemlock roots, are ferns, twigs, and blueberry rhizomes; miles of knuckle-notched tubes recycling nutrients. On every square inch of the tree structure grows moss or lichen, onto which land particles of airborne soil to create exquisite, hanging baskets. Entire bushes and trees sprout seventy feet in the air. Under the ground, mycorrhizae attach all the trees together in a network.

In this structure, there is no death of an individual. In the air and under ground, life begets life begets life begets life in the pattern of an Escher woodcut. A Douglas maple twines in and out of the old trunk. Gnarled arms gesture like a belly dancer. Seeds high in the moss reinvent their parents, no matter where they land. Because this old conifer harbors so much other plant life above ground and so many miles of fungus below and on the ground, it may take fifteen hundred years to complete its life cycle. Yet, as recently as the 1960s, "foresters" were claiming that old growth forests were barren wastelands.

The concept of "canopy," the upper layer of forest growth that serves as a habitat, is new to me as a southwesterner. In fact, it was new to forestry scientists as well until studies were begun within the last two decades.

When I was a little girl, the very first book that moved me from struggling along sounding out letters to reading eagerly for story line was *The Tune Is in the Trees*. The little girl in the story shrank to the size of a robin and went to live in the treetops, a career choice that held much appeal for me. The imaginative force from the story is still working within me and often surfaces while I learn scientific facts.

The continuous tops of trees provide an endless variety of surfaces, cavities, openings, and complexities on which billions of tiny algae, fungi, bacteria, and yeasts can live, feeding billions of epiphylls (existing on leaves) such as mites, beetles, spiders, and small beasties scientists have yet to discover. Together with endophylls (existing in leaves), this "scuzz," as it is fondly called by those who hang from ropes or rise in cranes to study canopies, forms tons of biomass at the top of the forest. Within one Douglas fir's sixty million needles alone is created an entire forest within a forest. Even more surprising, roots of deciduous trees can grow from the conifer branches out into the thick nests of moss and lichen, where they gather nourishment.

And from these tiny organisms that make up the canopy's biomass come larger insects, birds, and mammals, without whose voices we would not have a forest. Even the lowly cyanobacteria, liverworts, and lichens in the canopy are essential components in the working old growth forest. Not only do they provide pockets, dishes, and condos for the microfauna, but they are the only winter food for many ungulates. The three-foot-deep snow in winter will be speckled with bright chartreuse from the abundant *Lobaria oregana*, an essential food source to many animals.

☙

I am looking up as I walk. Suddenly I double over, hit the ground, and howl—as if the trees cared.

Pain jams up my leg. An upward pointing root, an evil troll, the cause of my pain, is cackling at me. I feel liquid heat swarm into my pant leg. I flop on my side, eyes closed, holding my breath, and think between the waves of pain. I hold my mid-shin tight in my grasp as if to keep my guts from pouring out through my leg. A new idea arrives: I could die out here!

Lying there groaning in the moss, I suddenly understand how an early hunter must have felt seeing his body sliced open by nature like so much carrion. Coolly, a scientific thought soothes me: I am just another belch in the biomass to be recycled.

The pain subsides, but my side grows cold and my leg, hot. There is nothing to do but wait for a while, using my hands to stop the blood. No blood seems to be oozing out. I am all right for the moment. When I can finally remove one hand from the pressure, I distract myself by withdrawing my topo maps from my pack and spreading them in front of me on the ground. Tree Farm License 22 BK4 covers the upper half of Meares Island and the Opitsat's sacred sentinel, Lone Cone. License 20 BK3 covers this southern lobe; bathtub-sized Dark Island is slated for cutting by License 22, and Wood Islets, by TFL 20. Lagoon Island is marked for cutting, as is the prehistoric sanctum of the Opitsat Nation.

Looking at these Forest Service maps is not helping my pain: Orange timber road lines writhe across them like varicose veins.

[Author's update: As of 1999, MacMillan Bloedel has put a moratorium on the cutting of Meares Island and pristine parts of Clayoquot Sound nearby on Vancouver Island. To appear to be a more responsible timber industry company, it claimed to be phasing out clearcutting over the next five years, avoiding logging in contentious areas and even pulling out of the industry's political organization, the Forest Alliance. By doing so, MacBlo is putting pressure on other, less responsible companies. However, their "variable retention logging" is very close to clearcutting.

In the late 1980s and early 1990s, when local whites and Opitsat natives threw their bodies in front of chain saw boats, MacMillan Bloedel sold TFL 46 to a multinational company, Interfor, which, under pressure from lawsuits, native claims, and the infamous En-viruses,[3] signed an agreement with the provincial government that required it to follow certain guidelines while being guaranteed less interruption from timber extraction. The cutting was stopped for the time being.

Following immense grass-roots efforts on the part of thousands of citizens, the mid-1990s saw the successful implementation of the Forest Practices Code. However, in 1998 Premier Glen Clark managed to plunge conservation back into the Dark Ages.]

The pain mysteriously begins to dim. On my leg a blue whale under taut blue skin has swollen up two inches high, thirteen inches long, and five inches wide. I cool my injury with wet salal leaves whose long

---

[3] "Envirus" is the term used by the forest product industry to mean politically effective, articulate citizens who are willing to put themselves on the line for the environment.

racemes of pink bell-shaped flowers will later turn to hard purple berries. I then elevate my leg on a forked branch and lie there in the rain with water pouring up my clothes. I long for an Opitsat medicine woman to drop casually by on one of her berry picking treks.

In the distance, a foghorn moans. In near darkness in a tunnel of foliage so low only wolves could pass without ducking, I lie examining my fears of the forest primeval. After all, the fear I feel should not be a factor for a contemporary human educated in natural history and having a credible level of wilderness skills. I have treated many children with injuries in the wilds. I am not afraid. Definitely not afraid. I get up and start shuffling home.

Tacked to a huge, hollow red cedar tree is the sign "BEAR DEN 1984."

After limping the two miles back, I crawl into my tent. Through the zipper slit, I can dimly see the giant bases of twenty-eight-foot-around fluted columns. I count my tree blessings: In one day, I have seen one western red cedar sixty feet around and another one reported as being fifteen hundred years old and still standing.

The distinctive red cedar bark is the Sears and Roebuck store to the native people from southern Oregon to Alaska. Though it requires real skill to peal it off in long strips, it can be used for making clothes, bedding, bandages, hats, weavings, ceremonial headbands, plaited plates and trays, twilled mats for baked salmon, cook-pot linings, canoe bailers, tinder, slow torches for travel, sails, and sanitary pads.

Cedar limbs are twisted into rope to bind bent wood boxes, to pull dead whales home, to weave imbricated baskets. Cedar boughs are used to sweep fishing nets after the fish are removed and the walls of a home after the removal of a corpse. Chewing cedar stops nausea during handling of the dead. Cedar also cures kidney trouble, breaks a fever, brings on menstruation, cures the common cold as well as tuberculosis, soothes soar lungs, and scours the body for ceremony or before burial.

Cedar planks support longhouses; cedar poles are carved into the totems that are essential to Opitsat culture. As part of the spiritual process, cedar scours one pure before whaling and chases away bad luck. Hollowed into a canoe, its enormous trunk carries men far out to sea. Smaller logs run the white-water rivers.

I am a bit delirious by now and begin to hear the native names for red cedar like a chant: "*t'sapi'stat, xatcatcl, pi'ts ohp, t'ci'tum, xelpai'its.* Even the Old English name, grand arbitor-vitae, means Tree of Life! I reach out to the forest floor and pick up cedar fronds full of rain to brush my swollen leg.

Night Wraps Its Tendrils Around Me

Night crashes like a heavy window frame whose sash rope has broken. High up in the canopy something cackles hysterically in a descending spiral. The tide rolls in until the water is only five feet from the rock shelf that holds my tent. I lie listening to dismal gulping noises in the dark made by the waves rolling up the smoothly fluted, glacial grooves like bowling balls. Heavy red cedar limbs slap the water. It rains hard all night long. I bail the six corners of my tent with a wool sock.

Forest and sea slam together rhythmically in the dark.

Morning, early. Ten thousand trapezoidal angels are flickering on my tent. They shimmer and skim all over the burgundy dome, reflected up from the water and down through holes in the canopy. A brilliant, pearlescent light. A tiny winter wren sings a voluminous trilling song two feet from my door.

I climb outside and stretch and stretch. The entire forest gleams, every needle freshly cleaned and gilded. Clouds stretch in rainbowed membranes across the sun.

Never before have I been so completely present or so joyous. This wilderness island, a black box of biology with countless wires looped together, is inextricably bound to my veins. Its interior is woven of dendritic wires in connections so complex that even a most brilliant multi-disciplinary team of scientists could not hope to unravel them all.

Feather boas of mist curl around the base of each sea stack. Like smaller versions of Meares Island, each of these small rocky islands contain its own perfect circuities of birds and plants and nitrogen-laden guano.

Meares Island cannot be chopped apart without losing fourteen thousand years of fine-tuning and twenty-eight million years of evolutionary cooperation and competition.

My shin is better, the swelling almost gone.

This fresh morning belongs to gull cries and sea breath. I am ready to stay for a long, long time. I can't remember when anything so wonderful has happened to me. Far off in the haze of the sea, an orange dot grows on the horizon. My heart sinks. Sharon has worried about me all night long and is coming early to "rescue" me. I want to walk again into the thick trees where parallel shafts of light streak down through the canopy. I long to listen for the howls of island wolves. I want to lie with my belly and chest on this island looking through my hand lens. I long to crack the cabalistic codes of its ancient organisms.

The Incredible Lightness
of Trail Building:
Clayoquot Sound

So I went on for some days cutting and hewing timber, and
also studs and rafters, all with my narrow axe, not having
many communicable or scholar-like thoughts, singing to
myself.

—Henry David Thoreau, *Walden*

48°15' N × 125°50' W

A stream of sweat is pouring down between my eyes. A black fly is
sucking my left shoulder in spite of Deet. Down narrow cedar
shake steps steep as an uneven ladder, I balance a fifty pound stringer
(a cedar beam) as I descend the mountain saddle dividing the Clayoquot and Kennedy River drainages. This is the fifth day of the hard-
est labor I have ever done in my life.

After weeks of traveling solo in the wilderness, I felt driven to join
a motley crew attempting to build a trail through the forests of Clayoquot Sound to show the world the immense destruction being
caused by clearcutting.[1] I am uncomfortable with all the camaraderie,
but that is the price of being part of the political system. When I drove
off Highway 4 and stopped at the plywood roadside stand displaying
posters and petitions, I was immediately accosted by post–hippie

---

[1] Since we built the Witness Trail in 1993, MacMillan Bloedel has placed a
moratorium on cutting the most pristine parts of Clayoquot Sound.

camp followers and almost turned to flee. Fortunately, an articulate camp organizer rescued me and led me up the mountain.

Tonight I find myself sitting around a huge fire pit eating a cheap spaghetti dinner with a crew of volunteers on the mountainous south edge of the Clayoquot drainage. The pasta is so old and the sauce is so cheap that four hundred thousand Italian grandmothers must be turning in their graves. I don't particularly like the looks of the fifteen other people who have gathered from around the planet to build the trail; after peaceful solitude, I am an ornery, odd codgette. My companions appear to me to be in their postadolescent, rebellious stages. Since my 1960s protest days, such scripts run boring loops in my brain.

Since May, the crew has included Suzanne from Great Britain, the vivacious Scottish sisters Dawn and Camille, Kevin from London, Kan from Japan, Jens from Germany, and many North Americans from both sides of the forty-ninth parallel. Anne, a physician, has seriously discussed with her children, ages nine and eleven, the pros and cons of getting themselves arrested and the nature of civil disobedience. The children have helped to choose this peaceful, if sweaty, venue for venting her frustrations.

"Why are you here?" a nineteen-year-old Vancouverite asks me almost rudely. My nationality and age place me under suspicion.

I think for a moment and then respond, "It's heartwarming to me, a Washingtonian who considers the forty-ninth parallel border to be a mad figment of our governments' imaginations, that citizens from other parts of the globe lavish such energy on a rain forest half a world away. I am horrified by the way most of the Olympic Peninsula's forest has been clearcut, so I really treasure these untouched northern counterparts."

The nineteen-year-old cocks his head at me and strokes his fuzzy chin, startled that idealism shows up in someone over thirty. Nobody offers me any of the cheap wine or funny cigarettes. Just as well, because I'm afraid that they would mistake my refusal for conservative thinking rather than respect for my body. But I do feel alone.

"All of us, of all ages, professions, and nationalities, have come here to live deliberately in these woods to learn to know ourselves better. This is a quest for all aware, caring people—no matter how old," says Tamara, twenty-one and graduating from the University of Victoria in environmental studies.

"How old?" Although I enjoy her nod to Thoreau, I wish she hadn't put it that way.

Grateful not to have imbibed, I stroll out into the star-strewn night, walk across the top of the mountain toward my luxury hotel, Die Fledermazda, and crawl in the back. Tomorrow I will face hard physical labor. I worry whether I will be able to keep up. I am also concerned about breaking the law: Soon trail builders may join the ranks of murderous criminals. The simple act of trail building on public land may become a criminal offense punishable by a year in jail and a huge fine. If the law passes and Royal Canadian Mounties arrive to enforce it, I will risk a $100,000 fine. I calculate. Whew, only $72,300 American.

The following morning, a wail from something that sounds like a krummhorn whose player is being drowned in hot oil awakens us at seven o'clock, we eat at eight o'clock, and at nine o'clock we begin to climb two kilometers and five hundred feet in altitude on a slum-ugly road to the landing area where the MacMillan Bloedel clearcut ends. There, Crew Boss Kurt Vernon has piled three head-high stacks of cedar shakes and stringers, which are split logs, that he has ironically, salvaged with permission from a MacMillan Bloedel site.

The work on our project began in early spring with Kurt scouting out the best position for the trail. Aptly named the Witness Trail, it will form a loop from just west of the high pass on Highway 4 to the road here, ten miles below, with both ends offering easy access to the public. Now, as September nears and cold weather threatens to shut us down, we are only two miles in on this lower end.

The first stringer I carry pounds down on my shoulder. Up and down, over roots, scrambling, pulling up with my arms, I am re-minded of the moves in rock climbing. Afraid of slipping on the wet cedar steps and falling eighty feet, I go slowly at first, clinging to trees.

I wear the first cedar stringer like a Penitent's cross.

By the fifth day, I am sailing over boardwalk, my boots are talking with the shakes, my feet are moving without me, lithely and confidently like separate animals with their own consciousness. I've turned into an animal myself, a simple, hands-on laborer, my mind having transcended any need for words by the seventeenth fifty-pound stringer I have hauled.

Kurt instructs us on the fine art of building a trail through twenty miles of rough terrain and deep rain forest. Extending from alpine lakes in glacial cirques, down two thousand feet into the Clayoquot Valley, and back up the steep V-carved valley toward Highway 4 over the middle of the island, the rugged trail will take a minimum of three days to traverse. Backpackers pass by us regularly, lavishing praise to our sweating backs.

This newest and wittiest bit of protest created by the Western Canada Wilderness Committee is called a Witness Trail because it is being built to bring the public to a site of potential massive destruction. A Witness Trail encourages documentation through photography and writing, and raises the awareness of the general populace who, in turn, can exert pressure on the government. I am drawn to building a Witness Trail because, as peaceful protest, it uses saws and hammers instead of chains or stones. My physical labor comes from, as well as improves, my heart and is far superior to long hours standing around waiting for a confrontation with police.

For the past twenty years, tens of thousands of citizens have worked to protect the B.C. forest, the largest remaining coastal lowland temperate rain forest in the world. Clayoquot Sound's 260,000 hectares (624,000 acres) of deep fjords, valleys, islands, and steep glacier-carved mountains are home to marbled murrelets, black bear, cougar, wolves, eagles, and abundant small birds, mammals, and amphibians. Its once abundant salmon spawning streams are still essential to the First Nations and to dwindling commercial and sport fisheries.

Meares Island seems so far away to me now that I find it hard to recapture what I felt so strongly there—to know at a gut level that saving the upper end of an ecosystem will directly affect that which lies below. When a stringer becomes too heavy or the flies too awful, I close my eyes and reenter the beauty I saw on Meares. Twenty-one percent of the Clayoquot drainage has been clearcut in an environmentally disastrous manner by multinational corporations. Thirty-three percent of its land base, much of it economically inviable fringe forest, rocks, and ice, is protected. With the *entire* ecosystem closely linked to the health of the ocean, we are working to save the land from the high alpine zone down to coastal bog.

Ninety-one Ancient Forest–clad watersheds of over five thousand hectares (twelve thousand acres) once graced the west coast of Vancouver Island. Only six of the watersheds remain intact. Only two are protected. The rest of the temperate rain forest from Alaska to California will be in serious trouble if deforestation continues at its present rate. Forests here will become fragmented into small areas if the 1994 provincial plan goes through; ecological health and biodiversity cannot be sustained if forests are reduced to smaller than a certain critical mass. Here in British Columbia, I have recorded many sites where companies cut right over rivers and streams, up almost vertical slopes, slashing and burning clearcuts so huge that they can be seen from the space shuttle.

A Minnesota backpacker, shocked by his first sight of Canadian clearcuts, stops to talk to us. "They're butt-ugly," he moans.

We few, we happy few, we band of brothers sharing bloody knuckles on the Witness Trail, are sorely aware of the great odds we face. Canada's New Democratic Party government invested fifty million Canadian dollars in attracting MacMillan Bloedel, once one of the largest slash-and-burn companies but now a bit more progressive of the companies in British Columbia. Both federal and provincial governments poured nine million Canadian dollars into public relations for MacBlo and other timber companies.

As in the United States, the timber lobby in Canada has millions more dollars to spend than do citizen protesters. Multinational timber companies have slapped lawsuits on citizens who have blocked their "right" to slaughter the forests around towns and native villages—forests that have sustained the people for centuries.

In spite of the odds against us, the grass-roots movement for Clayoquot Sound has grown across Canada and the United States and is looming large in European consciousness. In 1997 MacMillan Bloedel lost a multi-million dollar contract with Scott Paper of Europe due to pressure brought on the paper company for its part in degrading forest practices; the sum represented three percent of MacMillan Bloedel's sales.

Massive protests reminiscent of the Vietnam War era and blockades at the south end of Clayoquot Sound have been the largest and longest in Canadian history. Even though hundreds were arrested, charged with stiff fines, and imprisoned for twenty-one days, another two hundred professionals, mothers, grandmothers, and young people were arrested in the next protest. Around the campfire tonight, fourteen of us in various stages of exhaustion and dishevelment share battle stories.

"Peaceful protest attracts me," explains the newest addition to our group, Larry Dornan. Pushing sixty years old, he is a lab instructor of chemical engineering and a specialist in superconductivity at the University of Calgary. Bright-eyed and an energetic runner, he will have no trouble lugging sixty-pound stringers over the steep rain forest trail. I am amazed: He plans to spend his two-week university vacation donating grueling work.

"Why?" we ask him.

"To build something I can show my grandchildren—twins—who were just born. When I am no longer here, their Mum'll bring them up, and they will know that I've been here. I know that in five months this all may be obliterated by machines. But by doing this work physically, we are making a bigger commitment than with words alone. This is action of a greater order of magnitude."

"Why does someone from halfway across the planet want to work so hard on *our* rain forests?" I ask Jens Molter of Germany, a college student who has spent his summer on an exchange program working with the Cree Nation in central Canada.

"Za provincial government is lying to za natives to increase zheir receptivity toward uranium mining und export to Germany, und za return of nuclear vaste to za Cree homelund as dumping site. Za government compares zhis cycle to a Medicine Wheel—zhey say za recycling of lethal substance back into za land is a spiritual act. Zhey make horrible lies!"

Struggling to find English words, he continues, "It vas terrifying, za effectiveness of za industry und za government to act harmfully to za health of a whole nation. Native Cree people had no knowledge of za dangers of nuclear fuel dumping. Zhat's vhy I vant to make za Vitness Trail, so people vill know vhat a government can do to us." The parallel to German history is not lost on us.

Tamara Mortimer, a French Canadian, tells us, "I needed to do something really *tangible* rather than just speaking words. Here, more than I ever expected, I have invested more deeply and have been more deeply affected, more alive."

Others add their own comments:

"In London, protesters were driven up against a wall and clubbed."

"In Canada, we were dragged off and thrown in prison."

"In America, we file legal appeals through the Ninth District or chain ourselves to trees."

"Wherever we go in the world, we are part of a huge, extended family of conservationists," adds Tamara. All of us sit in silence for a moment.

Before I leave for bed, I glance around at my companions. Three people are cleaning dinner dishes, four sing to the gentle strumming of a guitar, five engage in heated debate about civil disobedience, and two of us scribble away in notebooks. With severely aching joints, I savor that profound tiredness that derives from meaningful work with friends. At the end of eight days, I will emerge from the forest healthier, heartier, and, I hope, a bit more empowered. I plan to drive back roads down the west side of the island, camp near Victoria, then take an American ferry across to the Olympic Peninsula.

I came to Clayoquot Sound to document the rain forest and to learn trail-building skills. Instead, I learn a powerful lesson in humanity.

Part Four

The Olympic Edge from Ice to Ocean Bottom

Mount Olympus's
Mighty Blue Glacier

48°24' N, 124°44' W
to 47°45' N, 124°26' W

I tempt the gods of Olympus and set out my sleeping bag under the clear sky. At dusk I watch in fear and exaltation as a mother black bear herds her youngster across the Hoh in my direction, catches a whiff of human on the breeze, and veers off upstream. I lie still in awe and respect, ready to spring up and bang pots and lid if she comes closer. In the morning I awake to the thundering roar of a turquoise river.

Twenty-seven years ago, an acquaintance drove me up from Berkeley, California, for my first glimpse of the Pacific Northwest. He was my young mountain climbing buddy, a social studies teacher, wild and free, inexperienced, beginning. The fan belt of his Saab broke on the narrow coastal highway, and he fixed it as Winnebagos sped by inches away. He had long hair. We were in love, but not with each other: Ropes, pitons, and sacred mountains belayed our unlikely friendship.

This time my approach to the Olympic Mountains was from the opposite direction. From Clayoquot Sound on Vancouver Island, I slooshed south toward the Olympic Peninsula down the macramé of muddy logging roads that parallel the West Coast Trail in Canada's Pacific Rim National Park. I passed the Carmanah Valley, famous for the largest Sitka spruce trees on the planet and recently saved from the chain saw by citizens from all over the world.

If I'd had wings to fly, I would have reversed the route of migrating hawks to reach Cape Flattery on the Olympic Peninsula.[1] Lacking wings, I rode the Black Ball Ferry from Victoria, B.C., to Port Angeles, Washington. If I had been traveling earlier—say, fourteen thousand years earlier, my ferry would have been a dogsled. Instead of a relaxing one and a half hour ride across the Strait of Juan de Fuca, the glacial trough dividing the Olympic Peninsula from Vancouver Island, I would have navigated a glacier at least eighty-five hundred feet deep. Today, the north coast of the peninsula has glacial till that was carried by the Juan de Fuca Glacier as high as forty-five hundred feet above the current sea level. I could have continued to mush up the ice lobes that led into the alpine glaciers of the newly formed Olympic Mountains.

The Olympics are one of the few circular mountain ranges on Earth: All drainages radiate outward from the central Bailey Range and Mount Olympus, which peaks at 7,965 feet. Jagged and capped with the largest glaciers in the Lower Forty-Eight, the Olympics are a chaos of youthful orogeny and tectonic testosterone smashing together young marine sediments and surrounded by a graceful horseshoe of basalt. The Olympic Peninsula's geological birth is unique on planet Earth. Distinct from the Washington or British Columbian mainland, the Olympic Peninsula was born as basaltic seafloor that flowed from a rift off the coast of North America less than thirty million years ago. The Juan de Fuca and Gorda ridges still pour out fresh lava several hundred miles offshore.

Ocean rifts extrude the youngest rock on the planet, which then covers the older, but much lighter, sedimentary layers. In this area, the

---

[1] In the spring, hawks migrate from the Olympic Peninsula north to Vancouver Island by collecting near Cape Flattery, waiting for certain weather conditions, and then, starting in the uplands of the mountains for altitude, flying the dangerous fifteen miles over the Strait of Juan de Fuca. In the fall, they take a ridge migration route along the North Cascades foothills.

sedimentary rock originally eroded from the West Coast when the coast ended at the North Cascades and later eroded from the young Olympic Range. These lighter weight sandstones, mudstones, and turbidites, laid down in turbulent water, punched up through the basalt like soccer balls released underwater in a swimming pool. Thus Olympus and its surrounding mountains consist of near vertical or overturned layers of hard sedimentation, the challenge of mountain climbers.

It is unnerving high in the Olympics to confront my self coming and going. To backpack a dramatic landscape in a formative stage of life and then to rediscover it twenty-seven years later is to stumble across a twenty-inch by thirty-inch glossy growth chart of one's own maturity: the losses, the changes, the dead ends, and the triumphs, what I thought I would become versus what I have become, the way I thought, reasoned, and dreamed at twenty-three versus a quarter-century later. For instance, when I first observed the sinuous, ropy-textured pillow basalts that form from lava flowing underwater, I was intrigued and confused, yet I did not look up information about their origin as I would today. Back then I trekked with a simpler mammalian awareness, sniffing, scurrying, and writing the occasional poem.

The Olympic Mountains have never ceased to confuse and amaze me, but now I am compelled to ask questions. I live more outside myself than I did when I first ventured here. I am more focused on living beings beyond the transparent walls of self. Back then, I was enthralled with love, adventure, and an imminent return to Writers' Workshop in Iowa's winter-entombed cornfields. I was frantic to collect every sensation I could. Eight years earlier, the movie *Zorba the Greek* had blown apart my reflective, Emily Dickinsonian character and changed my life. The dichotomy between Zorba the Greek, played by an exuberant, young Anthony Quinn, and the self-absorbed, intellectual English writer, played by Alan Bates (delicious!), enthralled me. Perhaps comprehending allegory for the first time, I recognized that both characters danced within me. No longer willing to plod along as the dark poet mimicking T. S. Eliot and dressing in black, I transformed myself into a female version of Zorba the Greek.

Here, above the trees, the Ice Age still endures in the Olympics. Extreme precipitation from the Pacific, two hundred plus inches per year due to the sudden sweep of clouds up from sea level to altitude, has produced the most vital glaciers of the Lower Forty-Eight, larger than those in the loftier North Cascades or northern Rockies.

This is a place of identity-origin for me. Twenty-seven years ago, on Mount Olympus was a most exhilarating place for me to meet my new Zorbian side. Writer, be damned—for a while.

Mount Olympus

47°50' N, 123°40' W

In contrast to Zorba the Greek, I had been created of ice, of a Victorian grandmother, distant and cool from feeling the lack of free communication from icy northern European countries, from white bread and sugar, from silence about bodily functions and about human emotional topography. Thus, at twenty-three, I found myself on Mount Olympus high above sea level impersonating an ice crystal. I described this ice crystal in a hardbound journal, one of the many I had been keeping since age thirteen:

> Precisely at 7,630 feet on the side of Mount Olympus, I discover myself as an ice crystal that has fallen as snow on the Snow Dome, been trapped under its brethren, and is slowly being crushed down the head cirque of Blue Glacier. In a few decades, I find myself at 478 feet below the surface, melding with all the rest of my neighbors until I lose my own margins. Near the center of the glacier, I schloosh right along—almost six hundred feet a year, an Olympic ice-racing champion. Soon, though, I get mixed up with a slower crowd in the lower layers. For one hundred years I creep along near the bottom thinking I may never find my way out. Enjoying the numinous visions that transformative stages bring, how I long to melt out—to revolt!
>
> My past history has had its peaks of nobility. Four billion years

before, I shot out along with sulfur from a vent deep in the Earth's new ocean. Several billion years later, I found myself squirting through a fleshy tube in one of the first multicellular animals on Earth. I then became part of a sparkling stream in China, found myself as a heated drop of water in Marco Polo's morning tea, and later sprayed back out over the sea.

This morning, I suddenly feel mobile, as if churning within the belly of the great ice beast. The mechanical energy folds and slides me along under the weight of a glacier, feeling the smooth polish of stone. Suddenly, in that flash between a solid and liquid, become a very thin patch of water lubricating the ice down the mountain.

Nine hundred feet above, mighty cracks on the sides of the glacier funnel rainwater down the seracs to join me. Together we swirl around the dark base of a nunatak. At five thousand feet, I fall off the mighty shoulder of Mount Olympus.

Nearby, I hear an extraordinary roar—billions of water droplets thrashing toward freedom. Two days later, at 4,600 feet, I just miss joining a mill hole as it spirals to the bottom of the glacier and instead continue through its upper intestines to drip prosaically from its terminal wall. There, dazzled by daylight, I behold a bizarre hologram: my human self twenty-seven years older.

This older self now stands on tiptoe, holding up a tin Sierra cup to collect that very droplet. In front of me a glorious turquoise ice wall rises eighty feet above my head. Scrambling up thirty feet to the top of a moutonnée, a glacially scraped, sheep-back–shaped stone, I sit sublimely in front of Blue Glacier 4,128 feet above sea level. I am pleasantly tired, having carried a sixty-pound pack for all but the last three miles of my hike to the glacier.

I drink the droplet down. Once inside, she brings us a memory— how my mountain climbing partner had separated from me reluctantly—I was desperate for solitude—and allowed me to walk up to meet Mount Olympus all by myself. It was not that his company was unwelcome. It's just that I was finding the care and maintenance of a male partner very demanding: Was he happy? Did he get enough to eat? What was he thinking? Hell, what was *I* thinking? I couldn't think.

I clearly recall my first glimpse of the towering walls and seracs of robin's-egg blue, lofty as a hawk's flight, stretching forever up toward Mount Olympus! A sloping ice ocean rising in graceful S-curves, scalloped with crevices.

At fifty, the eighteen-mile hike up through the rain forest was much harder than it was for my younger legs, but no less enthralling. Where I sit today would have been covered in ice twenty-seven years ago; Blue Glacier has been retreating since the early 1980s. In 1650 it surged forward, joined with White Glacier, and advanced until the early 1800s. Now, the glacier's terminus shrinks back upslope, as the ice melts faster than the snow accumulates.

In my first journey, I gobbled down home-smoked salmon and cold white wine given to us by Philip Hale, a forty-six-year-old champion sports fisherman of Vancouver Island. I remember fishing with him, thinking that he was so old. Today I devour Greek olives, pita, red onion, and homemade hummus, having hauled them two days and four thousand feet up for just this ceremony.

As soon as the food is devoured (and Zorba said, "I devour the world"), I explore the craggy west edge of the outcrop. Looking over the top, I suck in my breath and leap back from the precipitous drop. A near vertical drop-off gives a view four hundred feet below into a steeply descending, U-shaped canyon where a long tube of Blue Glacier is self-destructing. From underneath a dirty tongue of ice thunders a small, wild Hoh "river." Snowflakes that fell before the Civil War now melt into roaring torrents on their way to carve down through the massive rain forest.

Change is vivid at the terminal wall of any glacier. Some glaciers are receding, some are advancing due to higher rainfall from the warming and evaporation of the oceans, and a few are stabilized. Over the last ten thousand years, tundra has covered this mountain range as soon as the land was uncovered by ice. I am struck by a contrast: Up on the moutonnée, lichen and moss have barely begun to take hold atop the bare rock. Soon, though, plucking fog and nutrients from the air, the mosses will become nurseries for tiny hemlock and blueberry seedlings. My old lichen friends from the Yukon will lay down the crumbling basis for new life, but these are new plant communities, new associations.

Zorba gives me an idea about aging again. Human time is merely an illusion as we pass in a flicker of Earth time. Constant transformations are the essence of being alive, be it human or mountain or glacier or love. We each hear certain metaphors in our beings like mantras and spend a life walking up them or writing them down. I come out of the ice briefly, dance furiously in a circle with my arms extended, and then fall back into the ice.

The Hoh River Carving

The young and impetuous Hoh rushes restlessly between two sets of steep foothills in an ever-widening, braided river bed. I have descended seven miles down Mount Olympus, making my way toward the ocean. Cobbles the size of guitar amplifiers and huge trees pile up in river islands, attesting to the extreme and sudden velocities. The river wanders a quarter of a mile between banks. The cobble has been plucked from the graywacke bedrock of older sea sediments flaked with black slate and then hewn by the power of water to flat-ended ovals and laid out as river shingle until the next flood.

This evening, I sleep on the bank of the Hoh, so close I might roll in. Here, not far below the glacier, the Hoh is all waterfall and fury, but I need to hear the roar of the glacier cutting down to the sea. When my eyes are stolen from me as the moon disappears behind storm clouds, fear sets in: the black V's downstream become a vortex to suck me in.

I have privacy behind the fallen, quiet giants that lie at all angles on the forest floor. The fecundity of old forests is powered by all the microecosystems within the old growth logs. For twelve thousand years, these giants have reproduced successively greater giants; scientists have substantiated a clear correlation between the amount of old logs "recruited" to the forest floor and the biomass the new trees will eventually produce.[2] Merely two decades ago, foresters called the old growth ecosystem a wasteland.

The next morning the river washes my face, brushes my teeth, makes my coffee, mixes with my eggs and orange juice powder, and feeds my soul. It has rained all night long, but now the low oatmeal-bottomed sky is shredding apart, revealing octagons of fragile blue. When sun strikes the Hoh's surface, pewter turns instantly to milky turquoise as lovely and opaque as the stone.

As the sun warms the land, cloud scrolls materialize "out of thin air," plucked from the miniature satin pillowcases that surround each coniferous needle, and roil up the steep slopes to merge with the dark ceiling. No sooner does one batch merge with heaven than twenty more materialize. Backlit by the sun, they turn into brilliant scarves that gyre and dance like Shiva.

I am so grateful to this river. I must stay close to the Hoh: It is a ladder connecting my young self to my older self, one bank to another, the rain to the Earth, and the glaciers to the sea.

---

[2] Ruth Kirk, with Jerry Franklin, *The Olympic Rain Forest: An Ecological Web* (Seattle: University of Washington Press, 1992), 121.

The Forest Canopy:
A Species Democracy

W hile it is still early morning, I pack my tent and wander down the Hoh River trail through groves of Sitka and western red cedar nine to ten feet in diameter. A raven caws, and in my mind's eye I rise gracefully to join it, flying up amid the conifer columns and into the forest canopy. Mount Olympus and its Hoh River have sculpted vertically stretched cones of conifers. As I rise, I notice a succession of layers, gradients of epiphytes, birds, needle shapes, branch bulk, and mammals. Elevating 210 feet to the realm of the ravens, I tower over most of the trees. Instead of fear, I find exhilaration in the ride, tilting over to watch the tree species transform in shape and hue.

Then I notice that instead of competition for energy and space, the key here is cooperation. I've never been so keenly aware of structural cooperation as I am now.

Instead of a closed canopy, such as in a hardwood or tropical forest, in which every leaf competes for every chink of light, I discover an open canopy. The conical conifers appear to have arranged their bulk artfully, thus distributing the open space democratically among themselves. I can easily imagine all these characters at a round table back at the beginning of the Holocene, intelligently deciding what the future structure, branch distribution, and height of each species would be in order to maximize sunlight, minerals, and moisture throughout the whole forest. In an old growth ecosystem, the greatest bulk of the canopy is down low, in the lowest branches. Here in this forest, the young trees and naturally shorter species spread their exuberant spires without being shaded out by the lofty Douglas fir and Sitka spruce.

Far below me, through numerous gaps in the canopy, I admire an almost rectilinear criss-cross of old logs adding their nourishment to the forest floor. Rising four to ten feet above them, abundant berry bushes blush with fall color, and above them, in neat balconies of successive height, vine maple are turning brilliant scarlet-orange. The yew trees spread their bright green needles above the berry bushes to commingle with the young blue-green hemlocks. Next, the true firs, such as the Pacific silver, grand, or noble fir, lace the mid-story with powder-blue, scalloped layers that look more like ballroom gowns than branches.

Throughout, the tree-frog–green fronds and fibrous trunks of western red cedar spew up like vegetative waterspouts. Near them, the dark purple and dusky blue-green Sitka spruce raise their bulk heavenward, laden with their paper-thin bracted cones. The exuberant Douglas fir and Sitka reach the highest, but the old hemlock give their skinny tops a run for the sky.

On the way up to my present height, I was startled as the bulk of the canopy disappeared by eighty feet above ground. I had gone from dark forest floor, a soggy, cool climate, straight into desert. At eighty feet above ground, the sun blazes, the needles shorten and fatten, halfway toward being cactus pads. The lower needles stretch longer, flatter, creating more graceful fronds. They are so different from the sunlight-adapted top needles that they appear to be from different species of tree.

At the top of the canopy, the sun sears all our crowns like a blowtorch. How does water, which must flow all the way up the trunks, make it this far, up where photosynthesis is rampant. I wonder how the upper and lower tree limbs communicate. Up here, on the conifers' upper branches, the bracted cones fatten like sun-laden piglets. They will shoot down through the various levels—either by dropping to the forest floor or by being eaten and following various animal vectors throughout the system—and then travel far out to burns or glacier scrapes where new forests are required. The scissor shape of the red crossbills' beaks is a stroke of evolutionary-tool genius, allowing these birds to pry cone scales apart. Their jaws open wide so that they may stick their tongue out to gather aphids, as well as the nourishing seeds. A scatter of cone scales and seed wings on the ground often means there is a flock of red crossbills high above, following the cone crop.

How distinct these treetops are from the perfect Christmas tree shapes of forty-year-old Douglas firs. By the time these older trees experience their midlife crises, at around two hundred years of age, their tops are broken, grizzled, bare, and dripping with long epiphytes. Epiphytes, more than any other element except tree size, create the atmosphere of old growth: mysterious, lichen-dripping, contorted, an abundant habitat for raptors. Here, where the trees have long ago lost their perfect shapes, the anal-compulsive tree farmer need not apply. Paradise unfolds for so many species through this very imperfection. The timber assessor who still sees trees as very tall toilet paper will disparagingly dub these monsters as "overripe." The beauty of old growth is in this very hole-iness. Like groves of giant flutes, the old trees are riddled by woodpeckers, brown creepers, owls, and insects of all kinds.

Dancing in tune with the trees, the various species of birds occupy the different levels of the vertical forest according to some euphonious orchestration. In the top, ospreys, eagles, sharp-shinned hawks, and ravens nest and hairy woodpeckers and red crossbills feed. In the middle, kinglets and brown creepers run up and down the trunks searching for insects, while northern pygmy and northern spotted owls sleep by day and hunt by night. In the lowest branches and in the bush, the dark, tiny bodies of winter wrens seem to be made of the negative spaces between the branches.

Relatively few arboreal mammals conduct their lives in the canopy, as compared to life in the treetops of the tropical rain forest: The western gray and northern flying squirrels and the dusky-foot and bushy-tailed wood rats spend part of their time in the canopy and part on the forest floor. The elusive fishers and martens spread the seed vectors far and wide as they eat the smaller rodents.

When the lowest branches (some the size of trees themselves) crash to the forest floor, the Douglas fir regrow their lower limbs from epicormic buds. Due to the graceful stroke of an evolutionary wand, these trees hold within their lower branches multiple buds so that the new branching is forked and reforked, forming good platforms for perfect nesting sites.

Enter the marbled murrelet, arriving up to sixty miles inland to the nest platforms in the old growth, after spending a life at sea feeding on ocean fish. Did the old growth Douglas fir know to form branch platforms to house the murrelet? Who came first? The murrelet chicks or the epicormic buds? The endangered marbled murrelet, which we watched in flocks of twenty to forty in the fjords of British Columbia, has all but disappeared from Puget Sound.

Most enchanting, though, are those indicators of old growth forests, the epiphytes—the lichens, liverworts, mosses, hornworts, and fungi. At thousands of pounds per hectare, they churn energy through the forest machine as efficiently as any conductor. They expand with water, protect the needles from desiccation, and collect dust and minerals to form secondary forest "floors" in the canopy. It is those floors that, in turn, feed and house the creaking, buzzing, and singing choirs.

As I rose through the layers, I noticed that the cryptogamic world, too, is stratified. At the lowest levels, every square inch of tree seems covered with lichens: *Isothecium stoloniferum*, *Hypnum circinale*, and *Antitrichia curtipendula*. Curling along with the mosses *Dicranum fuscescens* and *D. tauricum*, they form thick coats on the trees. The middle level, with its greater light, supports wide "doilies" of *Parmelia*, *Hypogymnia*, and *Lobaria* species, which fall in great big lettuce-leaf shapes onto the snow in winter to feed the ungulates.

The multilevel fugue is not over. The canopy top is draped with long trails of *Usnea*, *Bryoria*, and *Alectoria* species. Osprey gather large masses of these lichen to line their nests.[1]

High in the canopy the ravens glide through the treetops, their wings whooshing like brushed viola strings. As I look down on the canopy, cones, cylinders, ellipsoids, and paraboloids spread or stretch through the forest's vertical score like juicy Beethovenian chords covering four octaves. Each individual tree, each species, functions as an orchestral whole that cannot be shredded without beoming meaningless musical phrases. Nor can one species, such as the brassy, fast-growing Douglas fir, be favored to the demise of all other species. Who wants a symphony of two thousand blaring trumpets all with the same shape, the same insects, the same diseases, the same few birds, and the same timbre, anyway?

The Clearcut

> *Sweet are the uses of adversity*
> *Which like the toad, ugly and venomous,*
> *Wears yet a precious jewel in its head.*
> *And this our life, exempt from public haunt,*
> *Finds tongues in trees, books in the running brooks,*
> *Sermons in stones, and good in everything.*
> —William Shakespeare, *As You Like It*

---

[1] The canopy information was extrapolated from a trip I took up into the canopy, led by Dr. David Shaw, at the Wind River Canopy Crane Research Facility in the Wind River Ranger District in south central Washington on September 17–18, 1998.

There were only eleven canopy cranes on the planet as of this writing, and only this one in North America. The crane proposed for the Olympic Peninsula was threatened with bombing and burning, and life threats were made to its scientists and their families. Loggers in Forks, Washington, perceived their lifestyles more threatened by the advancement of scientific knowledge than by the blatant and unsustainable clearcutting of the timber giants for the past eighty years. Ironically, the scientists, students, Forest Service personnel, and ecotourists who arrive from all over the world to study the canopy must sleep, eat, and spend money in the nearby towns.

Two days later I stumble out of the hushed corridors of great cedar, Sitka, and hemlock into a hot, noisy parking lot where I left Die Fledermazda. I must drive fifty miles through tinder-dry clearcut across Highway 101 to reach a forested cliff that sweeps the seven hundred feet down to the ocean. I need to understand how the forest zippers into the sea.

After days in deep rain forest, the clearcuts enter my lungs.

There were nights as a child when I was so asthmatic that I could not breathe. Sometimes I would awaken the next morning in an oxygen tent in the hospital, a safe but artificial environment. Years later, as I drive through the clearcuts of the Olympic Peninsula in Washington and the five-thousand-acre clearcut on Vancouver Island, my gut reaction is more than aesthetic repugnance; it feels just like awakening in the night not being able to breathe. That was before I understood the ability of the massive forests of the planet to oxygenate the Earth's atmosphere. Holding the greatest volume of life per acre on the globe, the Pacific Rim rain forest is essential for processing atmospheric oxygen as well as fresh water. The Olympic Peninsula's forest has a greater volume of wood and epiphytes per acre than even the equatorial rain forests.

Vertical Beaches

I prefer my ocean beaches vertical.

Much ocean edge above California is cliff. Pacific winter-storm fury erodes the rock of North America back to high sedimentary or igneous cliffs. A genetic memory of the bleak granite bedrock of Land's End, England, must call me to such difficult edges. I am about seven miles north of the Hoh River and forty miles south of the northwesterly reach of the contiguous United States, Cape Flattery, and am dropping over a lip of thick foliage.

It is 9:30 A.M. As if rappelling within a waterfall, I am lowering my body down the cliff on a waterfall of tree roots. Hand- and footholds, rungs of cedar root red in the rain, creak with my weight. I do not look down but place my boot arches carefully in order to not destroy the plants holding the cliff face together. The miniature water cascade has carved a jagged stone stairway.

This headland cliff is made up of Hoh Rock Assemblage tectonic mélange. Tectonic mélange is not Seattle's current Grunge band, a gut-turning soufflé, or high Paris fashion. It is the churned and folded jumble of basalt and various sedimentary rock formed when the Pacific Ocean's tectonic plate plowed into the continent. At the base of the cliff, this same turbidite sandstone erodes into evocative holes and pockets and spectacular tide pools. The longest coastal wilderness left in the Lower Forty-Eight, the Olympic National Seashore's cliffs, bays, young river channels, and isolated sea stacks near the rocky points team with exceptionally rich life zones—benthic, tidal pool, river mouth estuaries, and rain forest—fed by alpine glaciers.

I love the north-facing sides of these rocky headlands—their cliff's higher humidity, their wind velocities, and their tough food web of plants clinging to bare stone or slumping soils. The lip of the forest with its robust understory is lush with salal, berry bushes, and devil's club. Near the top of the cliff, western red cedar has gained its precipitous hold. Far below hover the dark bluish-green canopies of Sitka spruce gnarled by the wind, and below the spruce, where the cliff foot unravels in Pacific winter storms, the white trunks of red alder mend the slope.

Remote sea cliffs such as this one can be treasures, little modified by man or his four-legged lawn mowers. Because the cliff forests have not been burnt, cut, grazed, or roaded, they remain wild-feeling, even adjacent to the slash and burn Olympic National Forest clearcuts. Other than a few reports by engineers trying to shore up wealthy homes built in the path of ocean erosion, there are few studies of these near-vertical glades.

It is only seventeen feet down the rain forest chute that I push through the edge of one universe into the next, Alice falling through the looking glass. From the western red cedars I climb down through the Sitka spruce and the treasures they hold.

High in the canopy, the sound of wet fingers trilling on wine glass rims repeats and repeats on various bell-like notes building up in pleasing layers. By humming these trill-notes in a line of music, I find that the sequence is often made up of open fifths and minor thirds, like old Celtic harmonies or medieval chants. Chills run down my arms. These eery, translucent intervals of the varied thrush, and the entire lyrical thrush family, bring back fond memories of music theory class and the pleasure of building chords by understanding them. These vibrating single notes of the varied thrush always turn my marrow to jelly, then play upon my bones as if they were glass flutes. The intervals also bring up a profound evolutionary question: did pleasure in certain intervals exist far before medieval monks formalized them? Far before humans even existed?

A white roar vibrates far below as the surf pounds the western edge of the continent. Awe scrapes me clean and pries open my senses. Awe hangs out in steepness, in darkness, in smell, in the difficult climb. A spiritual adrenaline, it springs from the body, not the mind. It has my soul crawling on all fours. It lies in danger, in rock exposure, in exhilaration. Awe springs from the shapes of roots, especially when I see my own limbs suggested in nature.

Awe arrives in the pound of the waves. With a pulse that is slower than my heartbeat, the waves seem immense. I find awe in the syncopation where surf and pulse miss each other and in the rivulets of sweat dripping down my scalp.

Down the chute I climb as the creek passes back and forth under my boots. The logs that follow a level contour, and even those lying diagonally on the slope, hold soil and are home to everything that creeps and hops through this cliff forest. A root pocket lends me respite from the drop, and I balance to contemplate a huge red cedar log that must have lived during the time of Leonardo da Vinci. I stoop to grasp its slimy surface and glance into its hollow.

Hidden within is a miniature yet complete universe. I squat at one end of the hollow and shrink myself to the size of an eighth-inch spider picking its eight-legged measure through its obstacles. Here are gardens within gardens within gardens.

The seven-foot diameter log spans a twelve-foot tannin pool, then proceeds 140 feet into the undergrowth to where its top has toppled separately down the cliff, another 70 feet of grandfather tree.

The ancient tree tapers toward its crown, its wood disintegrating into red cubes and melting into the earth. Its natural chemical and mechanical protection from the slings and arrows of the outside world, the outer bark, is long gone. Still, the old log continues to thrive as a home for the myriad of beasts, fungi, bacteria, and microbes that will turn it back into a usable food for more trees.

Without these dead and downed logs, the whole cliff would be nothing but sluffing dirt, dry as a bone.

I look again into the logs interior. Where heartwood once supported lofty height, there is a canoe-sized hollow. Carved out by carpenter ants while it was still standing, the ancient red cedar now secrets one-inch ferns with cobwebs spread among them. Pale mandalas of lichen rise from the dark squalor in ruffled lobes. All the wood's a sponge—and a stage.

Each wood layer—outer bark, inner bark, sapwood, heartwood—protects and feeds its own bizarre cast of character actors. A flat-headed wood borer carves out intricate galleries. The dazzling golden-buprestid beetle, *Buprestis aurulenta*, scurries through the fungus in the log hollow like a metallic-green Maserati. These beetles farm their ambrosia fungus in galleries that, in turn, transform the tough wood cellulose into a nourishing treat. When they must relocate, the female actually transport the fungus to new chambers in which moisture is precisely balanced. If there is too much moisture, the fungus overtakes and smothers its benevolent beetle symbiont.[2] I imagine death by cabbage and carrots smothering me.

---

[2] Chris Maser, and James M. Trappe, Tech. Eds., *The Seen and Unseen World of the Fallen Tree* (Gen. Tech. Rep. PNW-164), Portland: U.S. Department of Agriculture, Forest Service, Pacific Northwest Forest and Range Experiment Station, March 1984, published in cooperation with the BLM.

Inside this old giant, chartreuse water drops glow brighter than all else in the dark. Each sphere's black center is surrounded by concentric spheres, each slightly lighter than the last, their edges concentrating and recapitulating the light. They glow in the dark.

The spheres are miniature factories of sun, strangely refracted amplifications of light beyond all reasonable brightness. Oddly large, they are too big for the normal surface tension of rain droplets. An epiphytic epoxy must bind them, holding the moisture like a treasure against future drought.

There is more eloquence in this log's decay than in an entire German motorcar. Here, there are no painful endings as in an individual human life—only the great recycle.

This old log is home to a whirring synergy of spongy recyclers, from the tiny actinomycete to the highly visible amanita. Even when I tear the log apart, I can see but a fraction of the fungi mycelia that run throughout the wood, three hundred inches within one cubic inch. My favorite are the tiny bird's nest fungi, *Crucibulum vulgare*, whose "eggs" explode spore from within a nest-shaped cup. The tasty *Pleurocybella porrigens* grace the fallen log with angel's wings.

From the perspective of a spider, I delight in the cream-colored carnations of *Ceratiomyxa fruticulosa* in fruit. Fungi are of utmost importance to the rain forest, ridding it of deep debris, freeing nutrients from the dead to be used again by the living, and fixing atmospheric nitrogen into a form the trees can use. Nitrogen and phosphorus, necessary for life, triple in mass as fungi and bacteria work in the old log. Moisture, a metabolic by-product, increases. The whole throng of gushing life creates complexity from simpler substances.

Because no Jean-Paul Sartrean spider has yet written in French, we cannot know the secret of life from a spider's perspective. I suspect it would be *"Fungi dirige toute le monde."*

Our arachnoid philosopher, though he does not hand me his five-hundred-page treatise, entitled *On Being and the Great Recycle*, leads me through the spongy trabeculae of decaying log. He patiently explains the many decomposers I have never seen before. Like a docent in the Louvre, he effuses over fungi who depend only on insect feces for nourishment and how these insects disperse the fungal spores. He describes this as one would describe the dispersal of Post-Impressionism throughout Europe. An underground art movement of great import, he explains, begins in the microbial world, which moves upward from the soil into the log as soon as it falls. Microbes turn waste products into nitrogen and organic capital to benefit future life.

Holograms within water! We stop to bow before water drops, globular lanterns of liquid green that look as if they will break if my feet are too rough. Twenty-five hundred droplets that, if I were larger, would appear as mist on cobwebs, but from this perspective look like the Earth as seen from space. In each one, pieces of azure and jade are caught and repeated twenty-five hundred times until my face blocks the light.

Out of the old log, once again my own size, I follow the stream as it tumbles the organic debris of a forest down to the sea: eighty percent fallen wood, twenty percent usable food, a burgeoning belch of carbon that flushes the forest's energy directly to the sea. What will happen when old logs are removed?

At last the cliff chute ejects me onto the bare rock edge of the Pacific. Jade green in the slanting afternoon sun, it furls with white breakers eight feet tall, intensely backlit by the sun: intricate Ming carvings serpentine with holes. The very atmosphere around the breakers buzzes gold-green with spray. I listen to the sea crashing, mesmerized. The sky opens up pearlescent with mare's-tail clouds. Beyond them, prismatic, lenticular clouds, gold-edged and dangerous, indicate high winds aloft.

I squat on the most distant jut of rock into the sea as landed sailors have done for centuries. High cirrus clouds mark an incoming storm, and now, on the southwestern horizon, a solid wall of storm clouds scuttles across the ocean toward me.

A Forest Swimming:
From Detritus to Salmon

47°58' N, 124°41' W
47°45' N, 124°25' W

*T*ide is the absolute boss at the Olympic National Seashore. In most places, weather, hunger, and stamina dictate when to move and when to hunker down, but here the explosive ocean is the unforgiving timekeeper. Giant waves now explode with a percussive wallop twenty feet from my body. My soles slip on the tilted layers of graywacke filmed with algae. Algae may be the basis for life, but it is not the basis for soles.

Waves carve the young rock to the point just below low tide and no lower. Twice monthly, exceptionally low tides just after full and new moons, called spring tides, uncover an area the size of a soccer field that is full of tidal pools.

My imagination dives into the submerged volcanoes and unseen canyons off the continental shelf. There, benthic upwellings mix with freshwater forests to create an eruption of invertebrates, fish, seals, and marine birds. The bird rookery islands offshore are out of bounds, a part of the National Wildlife Refuge. These coastal waters were exposed to oil development, overharvesting, and other disruptions until the Olympic Coast National Marine Sanctuary was founded in 1995 to protect 3,330 square miles, an area twice the size of Yosemite National Park.

From here north, rocky points jut out into the Pacific Ocean rhythmically every one to two miles, blocking the narrow beach passage.

Attempts to round these points at too high a tide could result in death or a terrifying wait. Desert rats, such as myself, do not at first comprehend that the tides are compounded by other forces out at sea and do not always match the tide table in my hand. A storm at sea, offshore winds, or a low pressure system will raise the high-water line. My exploration north of Hoh Head will be delayed. Tidewater rises, trying to trap me.

Huge waves crash into large, churning holes that are filling with ocean. All this scene lacks is Shakespeare's Weird Sisters cackling away in trochaic tetrameter:

> Fillet of a fenny snake,
> In the cauldron boil and bake;
> Eye of newt, and toe of frog,
> Wool of bat, and tongue of dog,
> Adder's fork, and blindworm's sting,
> Lizard's leg, and howlet's wing—
> For a charm of pow'rful trouble
> Like a hell-broth boil and bubble.
> Double, double, toil and trouble,
> Fire burn and cauldron bubble.

I've brought a four-inch by three-inch pocket Shakespeare with me and delighted in Shakespeare's sounds all last night. Reading tragedies by headlamp on a dark, stormy shore beats the late night TV horror show hands down.

Yet I don't like discovering the terror I feel within myself this morning. Waves pounding in such proximity reverberate deep within me, deeper than my skin and muscle, within my inner ear, slower than my pounding cardiovascular rhythm.

> Scale of dragon, tooth of wolf,
> Witches' mummy, maw and gulf
> Of the ravined salt-sea shark ...

Fear arrives under human auditory capacity directly into the marrow. Around these rocky points, sea monsters wait to devour female natural history writers. It is time to retreat to my forest's edge camp with a table and chair of log segments and ponder my coming isolation.

Freezing fog is rolling in from the open ocean. I keep glassing the headlands, where whales swim along the rocks to feed. The rocky headlands continue out to sea as eroded sea stacks, sharp, pointy little islands. The harder Hoh tectonic mélange contorts into arches and fins.

> Nose of Turk, and Tartar's lips,
> Finger of birth-strangled babe ...

Waves focus their power at these points, then dissipate their fury in semicircular bays. Steep cliffs of carbonaceous clays and silts interlayered with sandstone slump toward the sea ten feet behind me, an uncanny sensation. I much prefer the rocky north, where rivers cut down through the rain forest from snowfields and glaciers. In British Columbia, drainages become steep-sided fjords with abrupt vertical walls, drowned glacial valleys. In Glacier Bay, Alaska, the ice cuts right down into the sea. Going north is spinning backward through time to the Ice Age.

I love it here! One must be comfortable with one's self to be entrapped in impassable headlands that cavort like submerged stegosaurs with only their dorsal fins showing. In cities, I am not comfortable, in fact, lonely. Out here, bliss.

Near shore, another type of forest is recovering from man's hand: Huge kelp forests span sixty feet from the seafloor to the floating bulbs filled with carbon monoxide. Their long, tannish-red tubes serve as shelter, cafeteria, and nursery to many species. Sponges, nudibranchs, snails, whelks, and a myriad of other invertebrates find home on the stalks and sturdy holdfasts. Instead of fern and skunk cabbage, these forest floors are thick with sea stars, urchins, shimmering abalone, long-tentacled sea animals of brilliant reds and oranges, and playful sea otters.

The kelp forests, *Nereocystis luetkeana*, protect the shores from erosion. I watch two otters preen each other and tumble in the surf.

From only fifty-nine sea otters introduced in 1969 and 1970, their number has increased to over three hundred. The recovery of the kelp is attributed to them, because they eat its main consumer—the sea urchin. Their wild and magnificent shore is now honored by the rest of humanity as a Biosphere Reserve and a United Nation–designated Site.

Water explodes fifty feet straight up, then crashes back down on itself, withdrawing from twenty-foot-wide cracks with great sucking noises. When the water in the cracks descends twenty feet, it reveals pearly green anemones and bright orange and purple sea stars beckoning like Lorelei.

These crashing waves are reinventing life. Within the percussive wave, organic bits of rain forest are being pounded into the building blocks of marine life. Huge amounts of the forest run down to the sea as dissolved organic material, DOM, and particulate organic material, POM. Marine biologists studying energy transfer systems from land to water have only recently discovered that much of the organic material enriching the sea is not made up of wood debris itself but rather is a gluing of DOM into new particulate form.

In the crashing wave foam, a mysterious glue works at the gas/liquid interface. Sudden compression at the interface, such as in the surface suffused with bubbles, creates test tubes for growing new life molecules from another form of life, fragments of forest. Those pounding waves create larger and larger life-forms.

When I was knee high to a sea urchin, Rachel Carson's *The Sea Around Us* captivated my mother's imagination. Enticing me down to the tidal pools in Florida, mother told me that life began right there, right under my nose. It is now believed that warm mud or hot vents on the ocean floor were the chemical slurry that fused the first amino acids into what could be called life. The tide pools are the incubators for millions of young mussels, barnacles, sea stars, fish, nudibranchs, and so many other organisms.

In those crashing waves so near my camp, organic particles are snapping together like Lego blocks. Inorganic nuggets attach to those particles from the rain forest, gluing them into colloidal (gelatinous) lumps. Forming fibrils, or strands, they loop into bacterial clumps. These bacteria then feed the very algae that has been foiling my boots.

Although folk wisdom has long known the correlation between old logs and sea life, only recently have scientists begun to uncover the secret mechanics of how the marine food chain builds on the forest detritus. We intuited the flow of carbon from the land to the sea, but now we know specifically how the forest matter builds up new life material, how it moves up the food chain, and how, six to twelve months later, it is measurable as fish volumes in the ocean.

> O, well done! I commend your pains,
> And everyone shall share i' th' gains.
> And now about the cauldron sing
> Like elves and fairies in a ring,
> Enchanting all that you put in.

Benthic metabolism! Poets have always known bodies of water are alive. Now, scientifically, it has been proven absolutely true. The sea *is* alive. It has a pulse in the cacophony of waves and a metabolism in the health of its food chain. A body of water has a personality, a character, a consciousness of itself, and a sense of purpose—not just poetically speaking but within the perfection of the trophic spiral, the balances of energy within the forest-ocean.

Once upon a time, when the plants first left the sea, the ocean extracted a promise for them to send her alimony in the form of nutrients forever, so that, to this day, the trees are snatching off pieces of sun, turning them into carbon, and sluicing them down to the sea through log-stepped streams. Tragically, even under the protection of Pacific Rim National Park and Olympic National Seashore, and in spite of the suffering fishermen all up and down the coast, our forests are under siege. So many trees are clearcut in a strip from as close as a half mile from the beach to seventy miles inland that no trees will be left to send alimony to the ocean. The timber extraction industry behaves as the drunken husband who sneaks off to another state without paying child support.

> By the pricking o my thumbs,
> Something wicked this way comes.

I fill my water bottles with trickles from the cliff where bits of forest flickers off ferns, coats grass blades like icicles, and propels itself off mudstone lips in white tongues of foamy water.

> Boil thou first i' th' charmèd pot.

Giardia is rampant along this coast, so I boil my water for ten minutes. It tastes of licorice flavor. Somewhere up in those leafy woods, Indian licorice, *Abrus precatorius*, is growing.

How vividly I remember that roar of river out from under Blue Glacier. The Hoh's water was sweet and pure, running with rain's hot drill down through the glacial mill holes to underglacier rivers. Carrying only thin blades of sheered rock, "glacial flour," the water was filtered through trees nine feet in diameter. Into the water fell bits of leaves, insects, lettuce-leaf lichens, ground up birds, essence du marmot, and entire newts. Here at the coast, this soupy brew of liquified forest shoots far out into the sea, swirling on the Kuroshio, which, from here, curves sharply toward the Far East with the Coriolis effect of the spinning planet. Unfortunately for Asia, the eastern edge of the Kuroshio does not churn as strongly as it does here. Losing momentum, it creates less marine life. Asian fishermen travel farther and farther out with two-mile-long drift nets to scrape everything from the sea.

The current that surges out along the top of the ocean carrying forest detritus is matched by an equally strong bottom current that surges inland bringing the treasures of the benthic zone, nitrate-rich seawater, the endless fecal and algal wealth on the bottom, toward the shore. As a sylvan biomass is carried far out, the best of the deep sea flows back to shore.

> Root of hemlock digged i' th' dark,
> Liver of blaspheming Jew,
> Gall of goat, and slips of yew
> Slivered in the moon's eclipse ...

Above my camp, gaint Sitka spruce twist into muscular contortions on windy cliffs—jazz dancers depicting anguish, their arms flung out in one direction. Protected since 1947, this coastal strip of forest will mature into the giant hemlock, spruce, and red cedar forest that once was here.

I cannot forget that beyond this one thin strip of coastal forest, the metal jaws of feller-bunchers snap off trees like tooth picks; efficiency, not spotted owls, is stealing jobs from men. The change in the creek is obvious: silted up, warmer. A large enough block of coastal forest to provide enough genetic variation, feeding territory, and animal corridor is required for a viable ecosystem. Any animal needing to cross from the Olympic Mountains through the rain forest to the sea not only must deal with fifty miles of clearcut, but also must look both ways before crossing busy Highway 101.

Unimaginable to contemporary man, the Olympic Peninsula trees once crowded immense trunk to immense trunk; you could not ride a horse through the biomass. Now, some streams are trickles because there are no trees and lichen to retain water and capture fog. Others smother with silt and warm up the salmon that attempt to return to their spawning grounds. Layers of clay settle down to void out life.[1]

All afternoon, the atmosphere grows darker and darker. At 7:27, the sun briefly burns a hole through the corroded clouds. A bright strip of gold cuts across the cast-iron sea. A split second before the sun sinks into the water, a flash of chartreuse repeats the forest in the sky.

---

[1] Washington state's salmon fisheries were almost shut down by 1992; in 1996 steelhead fishing was on hold, and in 1997–1998 we fought the tragic Fish Wars with our gentle neighbors to the north.

Through a
Hand Lens Lightly

C hilly. 5:40 A.M.

I awake to the hollow sounds of a raven carving the Earth open with stony hosannas. I get up, slosh my face with water, brush my teeth, boil cowboy coffee, and stuff granola bars, tools, and books into a day pack. I'm nowhere near full consciousness yet, but I force myself to crawl around the tide pools on my hands and knees with a hand lens. Far out on rugged black stone carved with thousands of spherical sea urchin pits, I examine the camouflage of a lined chiton. Up close the brown oval is transformed into subtle hues in herringbone stripes.

Startling revelations begin in simple observations!

As in a healthy old growth forest, every nanometer of space is used: algae upon algae, fauna upon fauna upon fauna. I lie prone on a blue waffle mat exploring an exquisite, deep tide pool through a face mask. I am just about to give up on this pool when I spy something under a ledge, under the lowest low-tide mark. A weird bit of living surrealism.

Instead of appearing natural, this animal puts K-Mart's most outrageous plastic toy to shame. A two-inch tube of phosphorescent lavender glowing red from within, it explores its food with two handlebar mustache–shaped appendages. Two glowing red Rudolf the Reindeer noses pulse behind each antenna. From its back, inch-long, fleshy protuberances glow internally, illuminated in Day-Glo orange.

I know this is one of the wonderful array of nudibranchs we have along this northern coast. A nudibranch, pronounced "nude-ee-brankt," is a delightful tube of sea life that varies in form and color more than a Disney cartoonist can invent. I discover that this is the Elegant Eolid, *Flabellinopsis iodinea*, usually found much deeper in the water. Each projection off its back contains a slender gut extension that feeds on a hydroid, the animal that anchors the nudibranch. In addition to nutritive material, the Eolid absorbs the hydroid's stinging cells, lethal nematocysts and all, with impunity. Through wonderful digestive trickery, it incorporates the nematocysts into its own tissues, sending them out the long gut extensions on its back and exploding them on contact when another animal attempts to eat it.

The hydroid to which it clings is equally bizarre. An underwater animal impersonating a plant, the hydroid is attached to the rock with a rootlike holdfast.

Then, a more mysterious event unfolds. Interspecies cooperation is multiplied to yet another level. I notice a miniature shrimp atop the hydroid, its home. This amphipod is translucent; its red and brown internal organs appear as in a medical model. Much tinier than the nudibranch, it repels the larger monster with David and Goliath aggression.

Mother Nature's juggling act at its finest! The Eolid not only eats the hydroid but usurps its defensive mechanism into its waving points. The tiny shrimp saves its home by defending the hydroid from the Eolid and lives happily ever after, at least until the next great wave sweeps it into the sea anemone's arms. Three-way relationships become four- and five-way, layering the interaction of feeding/housing/protecting/surviving/reproducing between very different creatures. As I watch in bliss, the Elegant Eolid drops from its hydroid and swims with remarkably graceful U bends, reversing its body more fluidly than I'd thought possible.

If I have learned anything from this long journey from rocky tundra to giant forests to ocean ecosystem, it is the elegance of symbiosis. Symbiotic relationships seem to multiply exponentially as the plant-animal community stabilizes over the centuries. An ecosystem can be understood as a series of energy transfers from the simplest organism up to the most photogenic megafauna (bears and whales). We North Americans will spend millions of dollars saving one aging, male orca whale but ignore the bottom of the system. (Blessings to Keiko the Killer Whale, who has just been flown by expensive Air Force transport from Newport Beach, Oregon, across the continent to his Icelandic waters of origin.) Food webs are the complex, three- to four- to infinitely dimensional connections looping together the community, food being the mechanism by which energy is transferred through a chain and back to the beginning as the largest creatures die and return to the ocean or forest floor.

Yet, as global warming and the retreat of the Ice Age draw animals and plants northward, communities do not migrate together. The fossil record indicates that entire groups of plants that lived together in the past do not do so now. Instead of stable communities following the retreating glaciers north, individual organisms migrate at their own pace.

So what does this new development mean for my treasured concept of symbiosis? The fossil record indicates that virtually all different combinations seem to work together well—eventually. Life is incredibly malleable. Still, the success of each new ecosystem depends upon the efficiency and conservation of energy in the transfers. Ecosystem efficiency evolves over thousands of years but can be unraveled when man harvests even one species extensively or pollutes the system.

Natural disasters wipe the slate clean, enabling a series of new organisms a chance to develop a new symbiosis. However, justifying clearcuts by comparing them to natural disasters is like comparing apples and orangutans. Fires, earthquakes, and tsunamis take place for a short duration of time and affect a limited land area. Natural fires burn quickly through a forest, allowing grand old trees (with the best genetics) to stand and the mycorrhizal relationships to survive in the soil. Clearcuts and slash and burn do not; they remove *all* the trees from the gene bank.

I am enthralled by life's ability to recover, and to recover from natural disasters. Life arising from bare rock above the Arctic Circle. Krakatoa in 1883, California's earthquakes, Mount Saint Helens in 1980, the Northwest's extensive forest fires of 1995, the huge Pacific winter storm of 1996. All periodic wipe-outs open fresh territory for new experiments in balance and evolution.

I have been so absorbed with my tidal pool that a jade-green wave nearly dashes me into so much detritus. I glance up and suddenly realize I am joyful. I am reminded of a passage from *Zorba the Greek:*

> I was thinking of nothing. Rolled up in a ball, like a mole in damp soil, my brain was resting. I could hear the slight movements, murmurings and nibblings of the earth, and the rain falling and the seeds swelling. I could feel the sky and the earth copulating as in primitive times when they mated like a man and woman and had children. I could hear the sea before me, all along the shore, roaring like a wild beast and lapping with its tongue to slake its thirst.
>
> I was happy, I knew that. While experiencing happiness, we have difficulty in being conscious of it. Only when the happiness is past and we look back on it do we suddenly realize—sometimes with astonishment—how happy we had been. But on this Cretan coast I was experiencing happiness and knew I was happy.

I scramble toward shore from the outer tide pools. High tide arrives with a roar. One giant wave with the wavelength of half the Earth shudders to a pause and then reverses its direction. The tide feeds fishermen off Vietnam, thrills skin divers in the Caribbean, strands a yacht entirely above water in Glacier Bay National Park, swells under kayakers in Indonesia, and entraps me hêre, solo, on this rocky edge.

Tides are fascinatingly deadly. The farther north one goes toward the pole, the greater the tidal extremes. Where I stand, the variation is about fourteen feet. Near Anchorage, in Turnagain Arm, a drowned glacial channel, the tide gapes at thirty-three feet. The tidewaters rushing in on the south side and out on the north side of Turnagain Arm create a bore tide, a vertical wall of churning water four feet high.

I am isolated from other human beings but in excellent avian company. Black American oystercatchers mew loudly and tilt in perfect synchronicity to land ten yards away from me. I thought they were sensitive to human intrusion, yet they are oblivious to me. Has my dirt-encrusted skin begun to mimic graywacke? Does my clumped hair look like seaweed? Have I given up my human form?

Synthetic-looking birds with bright pink legs, red eyes circled in yellow, and red "plastic" bills six inches long attached to round, black bodies, the oystercatchers are proof of evolution's sense of humor.

Spirals of thousands of terns, gulls, cormorants, and eagles swirl in great cacophony around the haystacks out from shore. The ferocious surf that brings me fear brings them safety from predators.

To absorb the wave energy into my body, I climb up on an eight-foot diameter Sitka spruce log polished to gleaming marble from winters of storm. It is too massive to move, even though its end is out in the surf. Its shallow roots splay outward like Medusa's coiffure. In their snaky reaches hang macabre seaweeds, parts of lawn chairs, frayed ropes, dead bodies. The tide surges and surges. I lie on top of the log with my eyes closed. Soon the impact of the first large wave makes the log sigh. With the next, it shudders. High tide should be well past, but the water is still rising. A storm somewhere out in the Pacific is punching swells shoreward.

The upper log end is well grounded, so I know I can jump off. The waves keep rolling higher. Soon, the water smashes under the log into pockets and holes. The waves slam dance and gulp. Water keeps rising farther than the high-water line. I cling onto the roots with my eyes closed. With no vision, the rhythms of the universe, of asteroids smashing, of Earth forming, and of the Big Bang, all shudder into my body. The great beast wave strikes, showering me with sticky salt water. It packs under my log, which rises slightly on the wave's angry back. On my stomach I grasp two large roots as if piloting a rolling fishing vessel in a storm. The powerful sea knits and unfurls.

All alone, I gather in my long journey like a seiner does his seine and examine its treasures. I've navigated eighteen degrees latitude and twenty thousand miles. I've established a free-lance writing career, lectured, taught, researched, struggled with poverty and solitude. I've survived a whiteout on the Arctic Circle, skirted glaciers in a kayak, slept isolated on islands, climbed four thousand feet to embrace a glacier.

Prone on my stomach, I ride with John Muir atop his conifer in a Yosemite thunderstorm, drown with Captain Ahab amidst the slash of the great white tail, plunge into the ocean with Amelia, and dance with Zorba along the rocky shore.

Bibliography

Alaback, Paul B. "A Comparison of Old Growth Forest Structure in the Western Hemlock/Sitka Spruce Forests of Southeast Alaska." In *Fish and Wildlife Relationships in Old Growth Forests*, 219–225. Corvalis, OR: American Institute of Fishery Research Biologists, 1984.

Alaback, Paul B. "Dynamics of Old Growth Temperate Rain Forests in Southeast Alaska." In *Proceedings of the Second Glacier Bay Science Symposium*, edited by A. M. Milner and J. D. Wood, 150–153, charts, maps. Washington, DC: United States Government Publications, 1988.

Arno, Stephen. *Northwest Trees*, 223 pp., illustrated by Ramona P. Hammerly. Seattle, WA: The Mountaineers, 1977.

Arnold, Augusta Foote. *The Sea-Beach at Ebb-Tide: A Guide to the Study of the Seaweeds and the Lower Animal Life Found Between Tide-Marks*, 490 pp., ill. New York: Dover Publications, 1968.

Attenborough, David. *Life on Earth*, 312 pp., ill. Boston: Little, Brown, 1979.

Barber, K. E. *Stratigraphy and Climatic Test of the Theory of Cyclic Peat Bog Regeneration*, 220 pp., ill. and plates. Salem: Merrimack Book Services, 1981.

Bascom, Willard. *Waves and Beaches: The Dynamics of the Ocean Surface*, 366 pp., ill. by author. New York: Anchor Press, 1980.

Baxter, Dow V., and Frank H. Wadsworth. *Forest and Fungus Succession in the Lower Yukon Valley*, 52 pp., ill., photos. Ann Arbor: University of Michigan Press, 1939.

Bergman, Brian. "Battle Across Borders: Yukoners Fight Washington Over Caribou Land." *Macleans* 104 (June 3, 1991): 17.

British Columbia Environmental Report 2, no. 4 (December 1991).

British Columbia Parks. *Chilko Study*, ill. Prince George, B.C.: B.C. government report, 1991.

Brown, Reverend R. C., and M. A. Lundin. *Klatssassan and Other Reminiscences: Missionary Life in British Columbia*, 199 pp., ill. London: Society for Promoting Christian Knowledge, 1873.

Burton, Robert. *Bird Behavior*, 219 pp., ill. New York: Knopf, 1985.

Canadian National Park Service and Tofino locals. Conversations with the author, March 1990, and local signs and brochures celebrating Whale Week, March 1990.

Cohen, Fay G. *Treaties on Trial: The Continuing Controversy over Northwest Indian Fishing Rights*, 188 pp., prepared for American Friends Service Committee. Seattle: University of Washington Press, 1986.

Cole, Douglas, and Bradley Lockner, eds. *The Journals of George M. Dawson, B.C. 1875–1878*, Vol. 1, *Fort George to Hgwy Twenty to Coast!* 296 pp., photos. Vancouver: University of British Columbia Press, 1898.

"Community Dealt Out of TFL #46 Transfer Decision," *British Columbia Environmental Report* 2, no. 4 (December 1991): 19.

Cooke, William Bridge, and Donald Lawrence. "Soil Fungi Isolated from Recently Glaciated Soils in Southeastern Alaska." *J. Ecology* 47 (October 1959): 529–549, graphs.

Cowley, Malcolm, ed. *The Complete Poetry and Prose of Walt Whitman*, 538 pp. New York: Garden City Books, 1948.

Dunn, Michael Thomas. "Hypomycetes Decaying on the Litter of *Thuja placata*, Ph.D. diss., University of British Columbia, 1981.

Elias, Thomas S. *The Complete Trees of North America: Field Guide and Natural History*, 948 pp., ill., maps. New York: Van Nostrand Reinhold, 1980.

Ervin, Keith. *Fragile Majesty*, 272 pp., ill. Seattle, WA: The Mountaineers, 1989.

Farrand, Livingston. "Traditions of the Chilcotin Indians," Vol. 2, 54 pp., ill. New York: American Museum of Natural History, 1900.

Fellin, David G. "Effect of Silvicultural Practices, Residue Utilization, and Prescribed Fire on Some Forest Floor Arthropods." In *Environmental Consequences of Timber Harvesting in Rocky Mountain Coniferous Forests* (Gen. Tech. Rep. INT-90, 287–316). Ogden, Utah: U.S. Department of Agriculture, Forest Service, Intermountain Forest and Range Experiment Station, 1980.

Foy, Joe, Director of Western Canada Wilderness Coalition. Conversation with the author, 1992–1998, Vancouver, British Columbia.

Furniss, R. L., and V. M. Carolin. *Western Forest Insects*, 654 pp. (Misc. Publications No. 1339). Washington, DC: Department of Agriculture, Forest Service, 1977.

Gehring, Catherine A., and Thomas G. Whitman. "Herbivore-Driven Mycorrhizal Mutualism in Insect-Susceptible Pinyon Pine." *Nature* 353 (Oct. 10, 1991): 556–558, ill.

Gunther, Erna. *Ethnobotany of Western Washington*, 64 pp., ill. Seattle: University of Washington Press, 1945.

Harbage, Alfred, ed. *William Shakespeare: The Complete Works*, 481 pp. Baltimore, MD: Penguin Books, 1969.

Henderson, Jan A., David H. Peter, Robin D. Lesher, and David C. Shaw. *Forested Plant Associations of the Olympic National Forest* (R6 ECOL Technical Paper 001–88, 1–502). Portland, OR: USDA Forest Service, Pacific Northwest Region, June 1989, ill., charts.

Hilton, Susanne F. "Haishais, Bella Bella and Oowekeeno." In *Handbook of North American Indians*, Vol. Editor Wayne Suttles, Vol. 7, *Northwest Coast*, 312–322. Washington, DC: Smithsonian Institution, 1990.

Holdren, J. P. and P. R. Ehrlich. "Human Population and the Global Environment." *American Science* 62 (1974): 282–292.

Howse, John. "A Frigid North Pole." *Macleans* 102 (Feb. 20, 1989): 14.

Juan de Fuca Environmental Consultants. *Parks and Outdoor Recreation Division North Coast Study/South Section Assessment*, prepared for Parks and Outdoor Recreation Division, Northern B.C. Region, Ministry of Lands, Parks, and Housing, Prince George, B.C., October 1984, ill., maps, and charts.

Keele, Joseph, Dept. of Mines. *A Reconnaissance Across the Mackenzie Mountains on the Pelly, Ross, and Gravel Rivers*, 30 pp. Ottawa, Canada: Government Printing Bureau, 1910.

Kirk, Ruth. Conversations with author, 1992–1998, Washington State.

Kirk, Ruth. *Tradition and Change on the Northwest Coast*, 256 pp., ill., photos. Seattle: University of Washington Press, 1986.

Kirk, Ruth, with Jerry Franklin. *The Olympic Rain Forest: An Ecological Web*, 121 pp., ill. Seattle: University of Washington Press, 1992.

Klinger, Lee F. *Successional Change in Vegetation and Soils of Southeast Alaska*, Boulder: University of Colorado Department of Geography and Institute of Arctic and Alpine Research, 1988.

Knoll, A. H., "Patterns of Extinction in the fossil record of Vascular Plants." In *Extinctions*, edited by Matthew H. Nitecki, 21–68. Chicago: University of Chicago Press, 1984.

Kozloff, Eugene N. *Plants and Animals of the Pacific Northwest: An Illustrated Guide to the Natural History of Western Oregon, Washington, and British Columbia*, 624 pp., ill., photos. Seattle: University of Washington Press, 1976.

Kozloff, Eugene N. *Seashore Life of Puget Sound, the Strait of Georgia, and the San Juan Archipelago*, 282 pp., ill., color photo plates. Seattle: University of Washington Press, 1973.

Lovelock, J. E. *Gaia: A New Look at Life on Earth*, 157 pp. New York: Oxford University Press, 1979.

Mann, K. H. *Ecology of Coastal Waters: A Systems Approach*, 322 pp., graphs and charts. Berkeley: University of California Press, 1982.

Marchand, Peter J. *Life in the Cold: An Introduction to Winter Ecology*. 176 pp. Hanover: NH: University Press of New England, 1987.

Margulis, L., and K. V. Schwartz. *Five Kingdoms: An Illustrated Guide to the Phyla of Life on Earth*, 338 pp. San Francisco: W. H. Freeman, 1982.

Maser, Chris. *Forest Primeval: The Natural History of an Ancient Forest*, 247 pp., ill. San Francisco: Sierra Club Books, 1989.

Maser, Chris. *The Redesigned Forest*, 216 pp., ill. San Pedro, CA: R. & E. Miles, 1988.

Maser, Chris, and James M. Trappe, tech. eds., *The Seen and Unseen World of the Fallen Tree* (Gen. Tech. Rep. PNW-164, 56 pp., ill., photos, charts.). March 1984. U.S. Department of Agriculture, Forest Service, Pacific Northwest Forest and Range Experiment Station, Published in cooperation with the BLM.

Mathews, Daniel. *Cascade-Olympic Natural History*, 625 pp., ill., photos. Portland, OR: Portland Audubon Society, Raven Editions, 1988.

McAllister, Peter. Conversations with author, 1991–1992. Victoria and Seattle.

Meinkoth, Norman A. *The Audubon Society Field Guide to North American Seashore Creatures*, 813 pp., ill. New York: Knopf, 1981.

Miller, Perry. *Nature's Nation*, 289 pp. Cambridge: Harvard University, The Belknap Press, 1967.

Milne, Lorus J., and Margery Milne. *The Mystery of the Bog Forest*, 124 pp., ill. New York: Dodd, Mead, 1984.

Nabhan, Gary, ethnobotanist. Conversations with author during backpack in Arizona, April 1991.

Nicholson, George. *Vancouver Island's West Coast, 1772–1962*, 344 pp., ill., map, and list of shipwrecks. Victoria, B.C.: Morris Printing Co., 1962.

Nybakken, James Willard. *Marine Biology: An Ecological Approach*, 446 pp., ill., color plates. New York: Harper and Row, 1982.

Olympic Coast National Marine Sanctuary. "Olympic Coast" brochure, color photos. Port Angeles, WA: 1995.

Ovington, J. D. and H.A.I. Madwick. "Aforestation and Soil Reaction." *Soil Science*, U.S. Forest Service no. 18: 141–149.

Palm, Sharon. Interview with author, March 1990, Tofino and Meares Island, B.C.

Pelley, David F. "How Inuits Find Their Way in the Trackless Arctic." *Canadian Geographic* 3 (Aug.–Sept. 1991): 58–64.

Pelley, David F. "Pond Inlet: An Inuit Community Caught Between Two Worlds." *Canadian Geographic* 3 (Feb.–March 1991): 46–53.

Perlin, John. *A Forest Journey: The Role of Wood in the Development of Civilization*, 430 pp., ill. Cambridge: Harvard University Press, 1991.

Perry, Nicolette. *Symbiosis: Close Encounters of the Natural Kind*, 122 pp., ill. New York: Blandford Books, 1983.

Peterson, David L., ed., *Northwest Science: Special Issue on Northwest Forest Canopies*, Vol. 70, 109 pp. Pullman, WA: The Northwest Scientific Association and Washington State University Press, 1996.

Pojar, Jim, and Andy Mackinnon. *Plants of the Pacific Northwest Coast*, 529 pp., ill., photos, maps, and charts. Redmond, WA: Lone Pine Publishing, 1994.

Rhoades, Fred M. "Nonvascular Epiphytes in Forest Canopies: Worldwide Distribution, Abundance, and Ecological Roles." In *Forest Canopies*, edited by Margaret D. Lowman and Nalini M. Nadkarni, 353–407. San Diego: Academic Press, 1995.

Rhoades, Fred M. North Cascades Institute field seminar, "Life Before Flowers," August 1998.

Sharpe, G. W. *Western Red Cedar*, 144 pp. Seattle: University of Washington Print Company, 1974.

Shaw, David. Conversation with author in the canopy at the Wind River Canopy Crane Research Facility at the Wind River Ranger District, Carson, WA, September 17–18, 1998.

Sidle, Roy C., and A. M. Milner. "Physical Factors Influencing Stream Development in Glacier Bay National Park, Alaska," pp. 19–24, photos, maps, graphs.

Smith, Diane Solie, Curator of Atlin Historical Museum, author of a forthcoming book on Atlin history. Conversations with author, September 1995.

Smithsonian. *Handbook of North American Indians*, Vols. 5, 6, and 8, 800 pp. each, ill. Washington, DC: Author, 1978.

Steelquist, Robert U. *Washington's Coast*, 96 pp., ill., photos. Helena, MT: American Geographic Publishing, 1987.

Stottlemyer, Robert. *Managing a Biosphere Reserve Incurred Responsibilities*, New York, NY: UNESCO, 1971.

Swann, Brian. *Coming to Light: Contemporary Translations of the Native Literatures of North America*, 800 pp. New York: Random House, 1995.

Swanson, Frederick J., and George W. Lienkaemper. *Physical Consequences of Large Organic Debris in Pacific Northwest Streams* (Gen. Tech. Rep. PNW-69). Portland, OR: U.S. Department of Agriculture, Forest Service, Pacific Northwest Forest and Range Experiment Station, 1978.

Thoreau, Henry David. *The Maine Woods*, 325 pp., ill. New York: W.W. Norton, 1964.

Trefil, James. "When Plants Migrate: The Study of How Plants Moved North After the Last Ice Age." *Smithsonian,* September 1998, 22–24.

Twitchell, Karen. "The Not-So-Pristine Arctic." *Canadian Geographic* 180 (Feb.-March 1991): 53–60.

Ugolini, F. C., and D. H. Mann. "Biopedological Origin of Peatlands in Southeast Alaska." *Nature* 281, no. 5730 (1979): 366–368, maps, graphs.

University of Washington Department of Geophysics and University of Alaska. "Report on Recent Changes of Blue Glacier, Olympic National Park, Washington, U.S.A.," 6 pp., charts. July 10, 1996. Photocopy.

Vitousek, P. M., P. R. Ehrlich, A. H. Ehrlich, and P. M. Matson. "Human Appropriations of the Products of Photosynthesis." *BioScience* 36, no. 6 (1986): 368–373, graphs.

Vitt, Dale H., Janet E. Marsh, and Robin B. Bovey. *Mosses, Lichens, and Ferns of North America,* 288 pp., ill. Seattle: University of Washington Press, 1988.

Walbran, Captain John T. *British Columbia Coast Names, 1592–1906,* 546 pp., maps, ill. 1906. Reprint and update. Vancouver, B.C.: The Library Press, 1971.

Weiner, Jonathan. *The Beak of the Finch: A Story of Evolution in Our Time,* 332 pp., charts. New York: Knopf, 1994.

Wilson, E. O. "Biological Diversity as a Scientific and Ethical Issue." In a report from the joint meeting of the Royal Society and the American Philosophical Society, Philadelphia, PA: The American Philosophical Society, publisher, vol. 1 (1987): 29–48.

Wilson, E. O., ed., and Frances M. Peter, assoc. ed., *Biodiversity,* 496 pp., ill., charts. Washington, DC: National Academy Press, 1988.

Wolf, E. C., "Challenges and Priorities in Conserving Biological Diversity." *Interciencia* 10, no. 5 (1985): 236–247.

Zwinger, Ann, and Beatrice Willard. *Land Above the Trees,* 466 pp., ill. by author, photos by Herman Zwinger and Beatrice Willard. New York: Harper and Row, 1972.

Zwinger, Herman Hershfield, letters, 1989–1992.

About the Author

Susan Zwinger graduated with honors from Cornell College in 1969 in Art and English, completed her Masters at the Writers' Workshop at the University of Iowa in 1971, and her PhD. in Art Education from the Pennsylvania State University in 1974.

She has combined her interest in the natural world, her skills in teaching, and her talent as both a writer and an artist, in professional work and as a dedicated volunteer. Professionally she has worked for the National Park Service as Public Information Officer for the Exxon Valdez Oil Spill at Kenai Fjord National Park, and at Glacier Bay National Park and Preserve as a naturalist ranger. Her teaching experience ranges from elementary school to an independent high school to Assistant Professor of Fine Arts at Wichita State University and Colorado College. Her museum experience is both volunteer and professional; as a volunteer she served as a docent and workshop coordinator in multi-disciplinary approaches, and as a professional she curated contemporary art for the Museum of New Mexico in Santa Fe. In addition, she has written widely as an art critic for arts sections of newspapers and various arts magazines.

She is the author of three previous books, *Still Wild, Always Wild; Women in Wilderness*, co-authored with her mother, Ann Haymond Zwinger; and *Stalking the Ice Dragon*, winner of the 1992 Governor's Author's Award in Washington State. She has also contributed many stories, poems, and articles to magazines and anthologies. She lives on an island in Puget Sound.